SOUTHERN ELECTRICS SCRAPBOOK
Volume II

David Brown & Kevin Derrick

Strathwood

First published 2021
IISBN 978-1-913390-06-8

All rights reserved. No part of this book may be reproduced or transmitted in any form or by any means, electronic or mechanical, including photocopying, recording or by any information storage and retrieval system, without written permission from the Publisher in writing.

© David Brown and Strathwood Publishing 2021
Published by Strathwood, 4 Shuttleworth Road, Elm Farm Industrial Estate,
Bedford, MK41 0EP. Tel 01234 328792
www.strathwood.co.uk

The authors are very grateful to all the photographers, owners of collections and organisations who have allowed us to use the images in this book; once again, many exceptionally rare and interesting views have been unearthed. Interested readers are directed towards the Southern Electric Group, fifty years old in 2020, and to the 'Blood and Custard' website and associated Facebook group.

David Brown, Chichester
Kevin Derrick, Inverness

Above: A six-car train formed of two green-liveried 2-BIL units and a blue 2-HAL approach Barnham on the branch from Bognor Regis with a Mid Sussex stopping service to Victoria via Littlehampton, Horsham and Gatwick Airport (headcode '42') in March 1969. The concrete-faced substation building with outside switchgear was typical of those installed for the 1932-39 Southern Railway main line electrification schemes.
John H. Bird/Anistr.com

Contents

	Page
Blue is the Colour	4
Contrasts	24
Kent Coast Electrics Inside and Out	42
Tunnel Vision	50
Snow Worries	61
Passing the Box	72
Everyday Service	88
Side by Side	142
Towards Push & Pull on the Bournemouth Line	154
Specials	168

Blue is the Colour

The unique 8-VAB unit 8001 is seen near Shawford with a Waterloo – Bournemouth semi-fast service in about 1968. This strange unit was formed with vehicles from three newly delivered Brighton line 4-VEP units together with a rewired 'TRB' buffet/restaurant car, who's blue/grey livery contrasted with the original overall blue of the VEP coaches. The purpose of 8001 was to provide an extra unit for express services on the Bournemouth line, as rising passenger demand following electrification quickly led to stock shortages. Provision of three motor coaches was intended to provide enough power to haul or propel a 4-TC unit, but 8001 was generally coupled to another VEP (with its motors isolated) to form a twelve-car train. The motor coach adjacent to the catering car had its doors locked, was given tables and laid up for meals in a two+one arrangement.
John H. Bird/www.anistr.com

Opposite: The driver of 4-SUB 4106 looks out for the guard's green flag at Raynes Park as it prepares to depart with a clockwise Kingston loop service, via New Malden and Twickenham, in about 1970. One of the original ten 'six-a-side' units which entered service in 1941-45, an extra compartment was squeezed into each coach to increase capacity, making them cramped and claustrophobic to travel in when crowded. Some wag amongst railwaymen soon christened them 'Sheba's, quoting from a Bible passage concerning the visit of the Queen of Sheba to King Solomon, where she came "…with a very great train", a name which stuck. This sub-class had disappeared by the end of 1972, and not all ever received blue livery as seen here on 4106. *Mike Morant Collection*

Outshopped in early blue livery with small warning panels in September 1966 and by now definitely due for a repaint, 4-COR unit 3121 hurries through Surbiton leading the 13.50 Waterloo-Portsmouth Harbour service on a rather dull 16 August 1969. Throughout their lives these units, built for the 1937-38 Portsmouth electrification schemes, were known as 'Nelson stock' by railwaymen, both for their naval associations and the 'one-eyed' appearance resulting from the offset headcode panel. *Chris Wilson Collection*

Working solo, 2-HAL unit 2602 approaches Ford with a Portsmouth Harbour – Brighton stopping service in January 1970. The first 76 HALs had been built for the 1939 Gillingham and Maidstone electrification but were transferred to the Central and Western section pool, where they worked interchangeably with the 2-BIL fleet, in 1958. However, only one coach of the two had a toilet and the seating was hard and uncomfortable in comparison with the BILs. 2602 had just been painted blue and would survive in service until June 1971. The inverted black triangle on the yellow panel or end of two-coach units indicated to platform staff that there was no brake van at the other end of the unit. *John H. Bird/www.anistr.com*

With its driving trailer composite leading, 2-BIL unit 2134 calls at Gatwick Airport platform 2 leading a Victoria – Bognor Regis stopping service in 1969. A dedicated airport portion, generally an all-steel 2-HAL, would be detached from the rear of the train here. Painted blue in mid-1968, 2134 was withdrawn in July 1970. The cold-cathode fluorescent lighting tubes incorporating the station name were a familiar sight on new or rebuilt stations of the 1958-62 period. *Chris Wilson Collection*

Put out to grass on south coast locals for its final months in traffic, 4-COR unit 3141 stands at Lewes with a Haywards Heath – Eastbourne local service, on an unrecorded date in the summer of 1972. Headcode '49' indicates Horsted Keynes to Eastbourne but, as the Horsted Keynes branch from Haywards Heath closed in 1963, the motorman is possibly showing a sense of history.
Chris Wilson Collection

Opposite: Spare Kent Coast 4-CEP and 4-BEP stock took over from Nelson's on Mid-Sussex expresses via Horsham in January 1964. 4-CEP 7147 calls at Chichester with a Portsmouth Harbour – Victoria via Dorking service on 24 March 1969. At Barnham, the next station, a portion from Bognor Regis will attach for the journey to London. By this date a good proportion of CEP and BEP stock was in the standard blue and grey livery which superseded green and all-over blue.
John H. Bird/www.anistr.com

4-SUB 4126 calls at Woking with a Waterloo – Alton service in 1967. The overall semi-matt blue with small yellow warning panels was not common on repaints of existing S.R. electric units, only taking place for a short period in 1966-67 before being superseded by a glossier blue with full yellow ends. The white numbering was also smaller than the style later adopted. 4126 was one of ten all-steel 4-SUB units built with centre-gangway saloon accommodation in three coaches as an experiment before the arrangement was generally adopted following favourable passenger reaction.
Strathwood Library Collection

Dirt of the conductor rail has produced some spectacular arcing as 4-VEP unit 7711 departs from Eastleigh with a Waterloo – Bournemouth stopping service on an unrecorded date in 1967. One of the initial twenty 4-VEP units for the Bournemouth electrification, unit 7711 was delivered in the semi-matt blue with small yellow warning panels and cast British Rail symbols on the cab sides. It was very soon discovered that this finish did not wear well and repaints began very quickly. *John H. Bird/www.anistr.com*

Another 4-COR, 3102, calls at Lewes with a Haywards Heath – Seaford local service on 19 July 1972. The double-sided platform 4-5 is now out of use with track lifted and signal arms removed, but the redundant signal post remains. 3102 was one of the final 'Nelson' units to remain in service, being withdrawn that September. *Chris Wilson Collection*

Opposite: 2-BIL 2022 leads a pair of 2-HAL units, all in blue livery with full yellow ends, seen curving into Staines on 9 May 1970 with a service from Reading and Guildford to Waterloo, combining at Ascot. Another 2-BIL is berthed in a siding adjacent to the Windsor branch tracks in the background.
Chris Wilson Collection

Opposite: Early British Rail policy in 1966 dictated that all S.R. electric units, including the express types, should be painted overall blue, but only seven 4-CEP units received the early blue livery with small warning panels. These included unit 7108, seen passing Coulsdon North on the Quarry line leading a Victoria - Eastbourne service in 1969. This view well illustrates how the 'eggshell' paint used appeared faded and worn after a relatively short time in traffic and it was not long before 7108 received blue and grey with full yellow ends. *Chris Wilson Collection*

Led by 7707, three of the new 4-VEP units for stopping services on the Bournemouth line form an evening peak service out of Waterloo on 3 July 1967, having just passed Wimbledon. When new and clean, the 'monastic blue' livery looked smart, set off by the raised aluminium double arrows. By the time they entered service, the small yellow warning panels had already been superseded by full yellow ends on the most recent repaints. Wimbledon goods yard is very busy, mainly with coal traffic to Tolworth and Chessington. *Brian Stephenson*

Not a particularly usual sight, 4-VEP unit 7706, another of the original twenty Bournemouth line units, has escaped onto the Central Division and passes South Croydon with a Brighton – Victoria via Redhill stopping service in July 1969. Having been in service for two years, the original semi-matt blue paintwork has worn and faded badly. Blue-painted window frames, rather than bare aluminium, were a feature of most of this initial batch of VEPs. *Brian Stephenson*

Opposite: 4-COR 3153, an early repaint in glossy blue with full yellow ends, leads a COR + GRI + COR formation through Clapham Cutting with an afternoon Waterloo – Portsmouth service on Saturday 1 July 1967. Headcode '5' indicates that it will be routed via Cobham and will terminate at Portsmouth & Southsea. The shiny yellow front would not remain clean for long, particularly on the gangway rubbing plate. *Brian Stephenson*

B.R.-type 2-HAP 6041 was another early blue repaint with small warning panels and is seen here leading a Charing Cross – Sevenoaks service at Shoreham Lane, just north of its destination, in September 1967. The HAPs were a post-war development of the 2-HAL concept and were built in quantity at Eastleigh in 1957-63, mainly for the Kent Coast electrification. **Colour Rail**

Opposite: Another all-blue 4-CEP unit, this time in the later glossy finish with full yellow ends, 7198 arrives at Shepherds Well with a Victoria – Dover Priory service on 2 March 1968. Behind are the exchange sidings to the former East Kent Light Railway, where a KA type 3 diesel and a JB electro-diesel await their next duties. The E.K.L.R., one of Colonel Stephen's projects, connected Tilmanstone Colliery to the railway network through the curiously named Golgotha tunnel. **Brian Stephenson**

Opposite: Two of the three solid-looking Co-Co 'booster' electric locomotives, 20001 and 20002, are seen parked in Brighton station in January 1969, having just been withdrawn from service. A collaboration between the Southern Railway and English Electric, they were designed for heavy freight haulage on the third-rail network, but the intended series production never materialised. 20001 had been outshopped in blue to haul the Royal Train on Derby Day 1968, but 20002 remained in green to the end. With their domed roofs and welded construction, the cab fronts bear a strong family resemblance to 2-HAL electric stock. The class were colloquially known as 'Hornby's, for obvious reasons. ***Chris Wilson Collection***

On one of its final revenue-earning freight duties, blue-liveried 'Hornby' Co-Co electric locomotive 20001 is hauling a sizable load as it heads down the Brighton line south of Clayton tunnel on 1 January 1969. Although generally reliable and built to last, with declining freight traffic this small non-standard class had no chance of survival under the B.R. 1968 National Traction Plan. ***John H. Bird/www.anistr.com***

Opposite: Another of the early blue repaints with small warning panels, S.R.-type 2-HAP unit 5610 leads an eight-car train of HAP stock arriving at Bromley South with an Ashford - Maidstone East - Victoria stopping service on 11 March 1967. These units were built on the pre-war underframes of withdrawn 2-NOL stock and therefore had Bulleid-style bodywork, with the motor coaches being virtually identical to those of 4-EPBs. However, like all post-1951 semi fast and express electric stock, the motors were geared to allow speeds of up to 90mph. *Brian Stephenson*

4-VEP units 7702 and 7721 are seen between Lymington Junction and Sway forming the 08.43 Waterloo – Bournemouth stopping service on 19 August 1969. Although in traffic for barely two years, 7702 has already just been repainted in the glossier blue with full yellow ends and in the process has lost its aluminium double arrows. With their suburban-style high-density seating and doors to each bay, the VEPs were disparagingly dubbed '4 SUBs with corridors' by railway staff.
John H. Bird/www.anistr.com

Contrasts

The motorman is changing ends as an eight-car SUB formation waits at a largely deserted Cannon Street on Saturday 11 September 1954, the gaunt framework of the glass-less overall roof throwing an interesting arrangement of shadows across the train. Nearest is 4314, a 'short-frame' 1925 unit (originally 1299) with added wide-body trailer 10389. The distinctive 'bullet' cab ends were intended to match those of the original L.S.W.R. units but the unpanelled slab sides were of pure S.E.C.R. Ashford style, being designed by Lionel Lynes. *Alan A. Jackson/Chris Wilson Collection*

This slightly later view of Cannon street dates from 30 May 1958, by which time platform lengthening and track rearrangement for the 'ten-car scheme' had been completed and most South Eastern suburban services were operated by EPB stock. S.R.-type 4-EPB unit 5076 departs from platform 4 with a Dartford service via Sidcup but not calling at Lewisham while, to its left, rebuilt 'West Country' light pacific 34013 'Okehampton' simmers at the head of a Kent Coast express. The redundant roof framework, for so long a familiar City landmark, would be dismantled later that year.
R.C. Riley/The Transport Treasury

The Kent Coast electrification bought a new style to signal-box architecture, also seen on other parts of B.R. While clearly modelled on the S.R. 'glasshouse' type, there were no curved elevations and the panels above and below the windows were finished in light pastel shades. The new box at Rochester was close to the old cabin at Chatham Goods sidings, which it displaced, and the pair were photographed on 13 June 1959. Note also the electrical feeder and substation remote-control cables located in concrete trunking cranked-up to pass along a steel bridge parapet.
J.J. Smith/Bluebell Railway Archive

Opposite: 4-SUB units with pre-grouping wooden bodywork survived in everyday service until 1960. 4506 was one of twenty units of mainly L.B.S.C.R. origin retained for longer than originally intended to cover for the early withdrawal of the 2-NOL class and could be seen on most parts of the S.R. suburban network. Here it departs from Sutton with a Victoria – West Croydon – Epsom Downs service (headcode 'S' with dot) on an unrecorded date in about 1959. The diminutive wooden 'C' box, perched on platform 3, adds additional atmosphere to the scene. From 1925 until 1929 the lines through these platforms had been electrified on the 6700V A.C. 'overhead' system.
Chris Wilson Collection

Phase I of the Kent Coast electrification included the branch from Sittingbourne to Sheerness, which crossed from the mainland onto the Isle of Sheppey over the Swale Bridge, which was also the only means of road access to the island. It included a bascule lifting section which could be raised to allow shipping to pass. The line over the old bridge was electrified and equipped with colour-light signalling, and still used when the new services started on Monday 15 June 1959. The replacement Queensferry Bridge, a seven-span ferro-concrete structure with a central vertical-lift section seen on the left, came into use on 20 April 1960, when the old bridge was closed and soon demolished. A new concrete platform on the diversion was also built to replace the wooden platform named Swale Halt on the old line, seen here on 9 April 1960. There was no locality named Swale, and the halt was provided purely for the benefit of railway staff and workers at the nearby Ridham Dock. *J.J. Smith/Bluebell Railway Archive*

Another view from a slightly different location shows the old Swale Halt, built entirely of timber, and lifting bridge in greater detail.
J.J. Smith/Bluebell Railway Archive

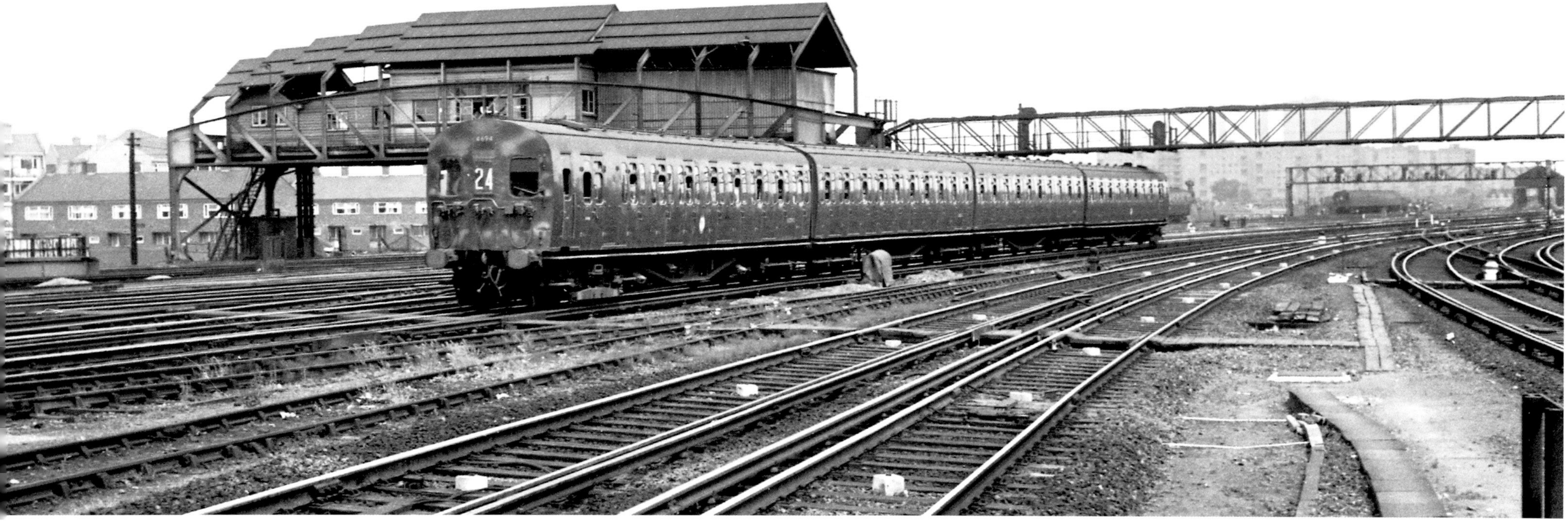
24

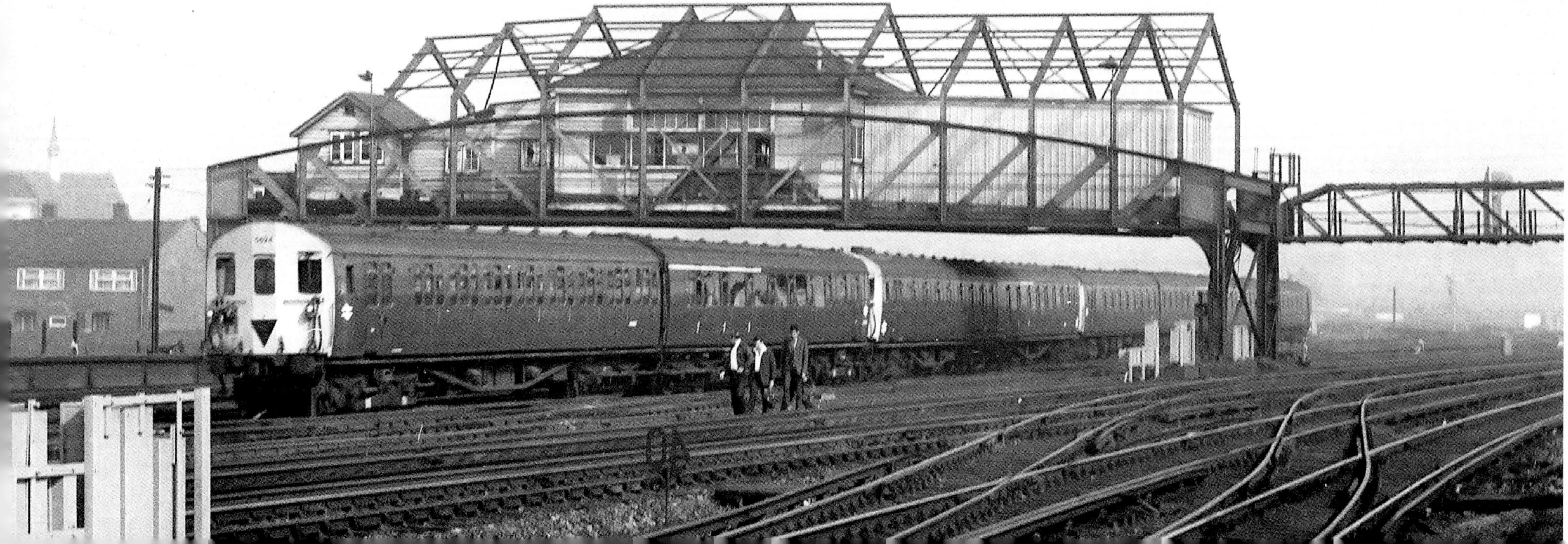

Opposite Top: Seen from the London end of the down fast Central Section line serving platform 13 at Clapham Junction, 4 SUB 4694 approaches on the South Western main suburban line with a Waterloo – Shepperton service in 1962. The overhead 'A' signalbox, which came into use in 1912 and was re-equipped in 1937, spanned the Windsor lines and controlled all the S.W. tracks at this point. The protective roof to deflect incendiaries on its substantial steel supporting frame was added at the start of World War Two. Bottom: S.R.-type 2-HAP 5624 departs from Clapham Junction on the rear of a Waterloo-bound service on a misty day in 1970. In 1965 the blast-roof partially collapsed, causing much disruption, and was quickly removed. The cause was found to be corrosion of the supporting steelwork in one particular place, the result of generations of signalmen throwing their tea-pot dregs out of the same window. High-visibility orange vests were coming into use at this time, but their use appears to be entirely optional.
Both: Chris Wilson Collection

Above: This view dates from about 1966, shortly after the blast-roof was removed from 'A' box. 2-HAL 2634 leads one of the two Bullied-type 4-LAVs (of exactly the same design as the HALs) slowing to call at Clapham Junction platform 13 with a Victoria – Brighton semi-fast service. In the background, Ivatt class 2 2-6-2T 41304 passes light under the box, probably to take empty stock from Clapham Yard to Waterloo. As a further point of interest, George Ivatt was Oliver Bulleid's brother-in-law. *Patrick Russell/Rail Archive Stephenson*

Opposite: An eight-car train of 2-BIL and HAL stock gets the green flag and is about to set off from Bedhampton Halt with a Waterloo – Portsmouth & Southsea stopping service. This was another very quiet station on the west coast line to Portsmouth, and was served by stopping services to and from both Brighton and Waterloo. In contrast, commuters alight from an evening rush-hour service out of London at Bexleyheath in about 1958. Persistent overcrowding on South Eastern suburban routes led to the introduction of ten-car trains from 1954, a significant investment involving platform extensions, power-supply upgrading and additional rolling stock. The new all-steel EPB stock had greater capacity than the pre-war suburban trains and most seating was in open saloons, which greatly improved travelling conditions. The advantage of a door to each compartment or seating-bay is apparent. *Photos: John H. Bird/www.anistr.com & David Brown Collection*

On the Central Section coastal electrifications of 1933-38, trains stopped at what had been simple rail-motor halts with passengers buying tickets on board the trains. To enable electric trains to call they were converted into stations, platforms being lengthened and ticket-issuing facilities provided. Southbourne, between Chichester and Havant, was improved for the 1938 Mid-Sussex scheme with simple ticket office and waiting room huts clad in corrugated iron. The original wooden platform structure of the halt has been retained, but the lengthy platform extension beyond the huts is resting on concrete piers. *The Lens of Sutton Association*

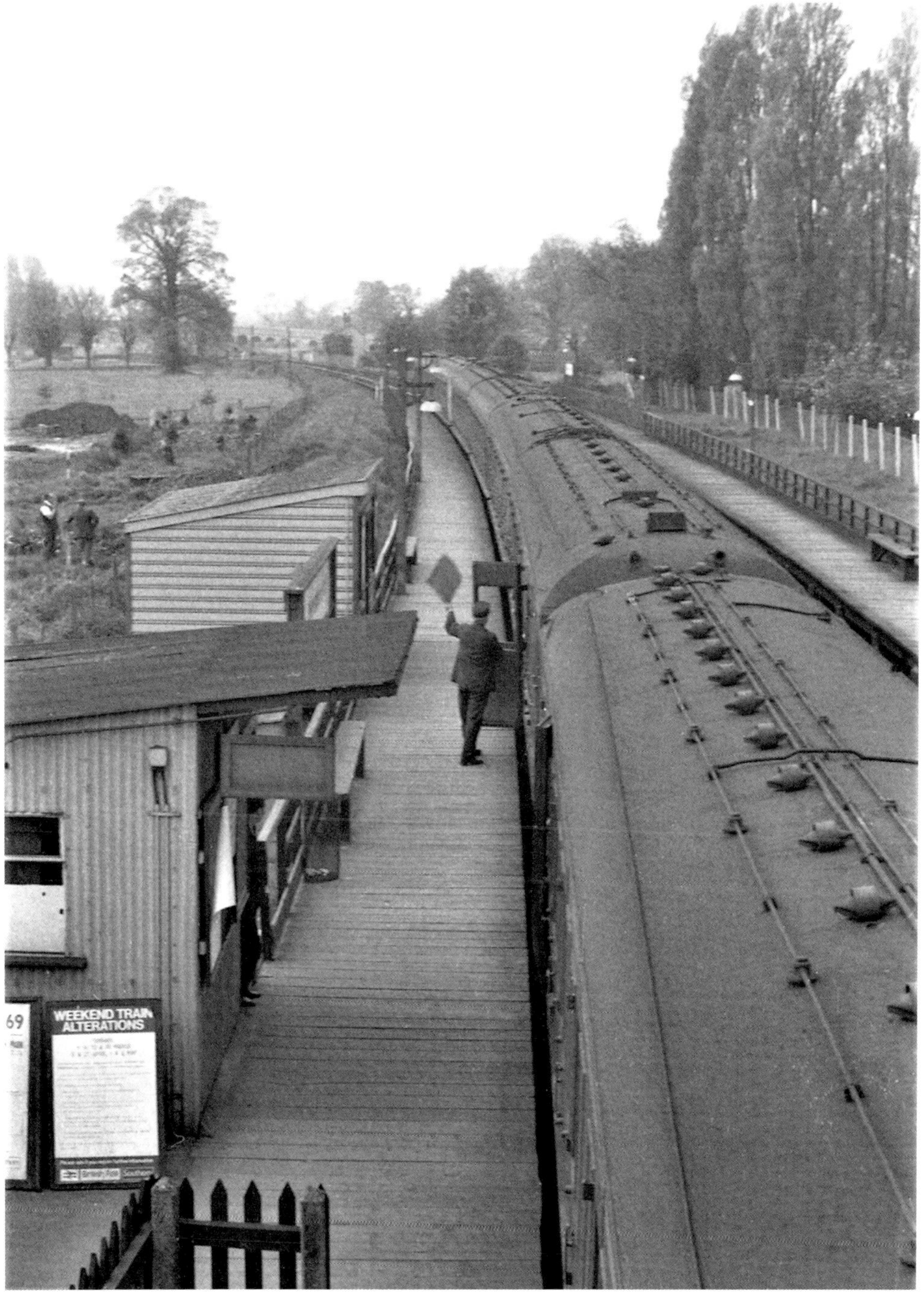
WEEKEND TRAIN
ALTERATIONS

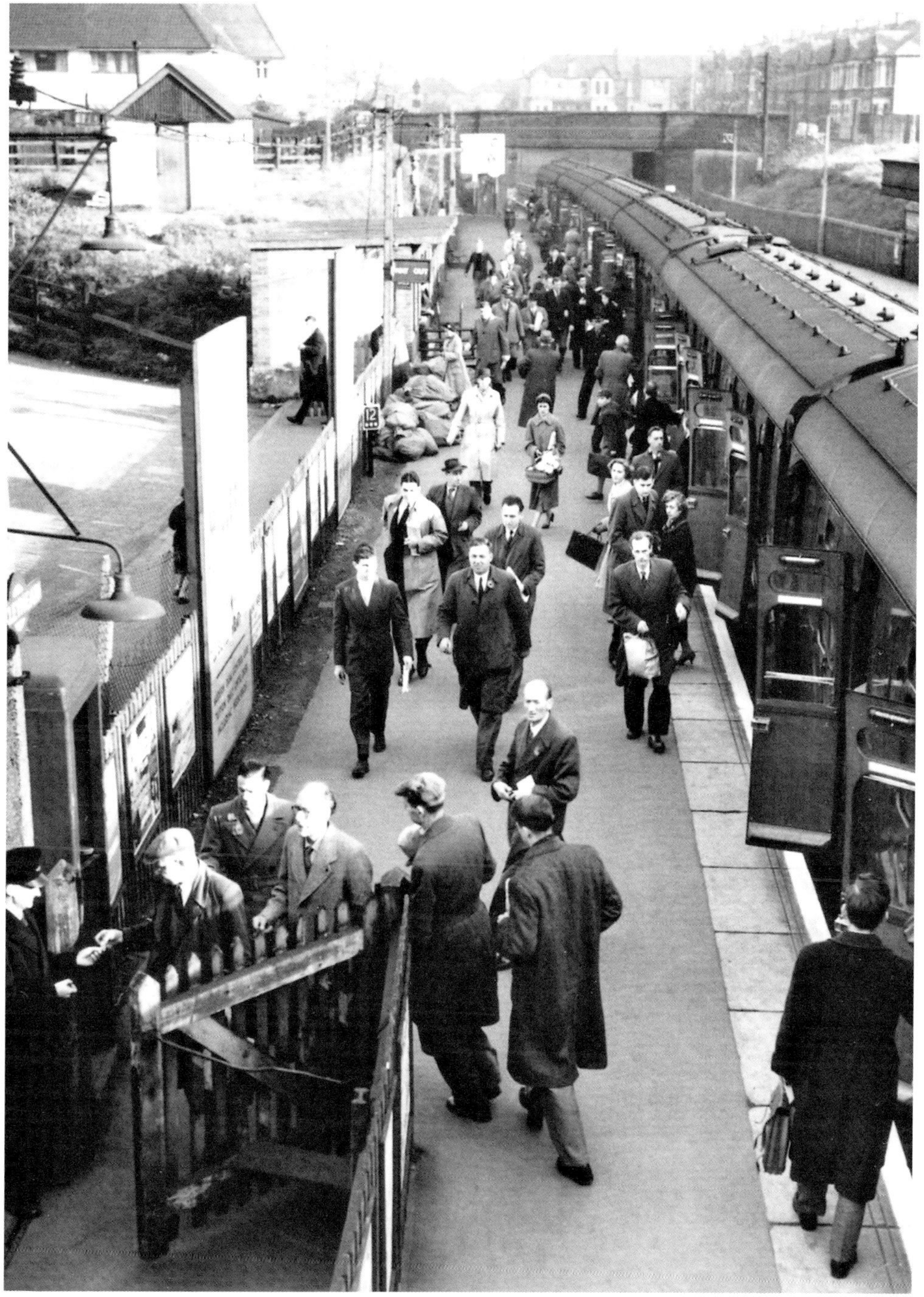

In order to fit more passengers into an eight-coach train which still fitted the British loading gauge, particularly for the congested suburban routes out of Charing Cross and Cannon Street to Dartford, Bulleid devised an arrangement with interleaved high- and low-level compartments, possibly using the design of a pre-war Rome bus as inspiration. Two experimental suburban units were built at Eastleigh in 1949 to test the design; they were classified 4DD and numbered 4001-2. For various reasons the concept was a failure, leaving the Southern Region no choice but to instigate the expensive 'ten-car scheme' as described already. At Dartford on a rainy day in January 1969 the compartment arrangements of a 4-EPB in the foreground and 4-DD behind may be compared. From the front the driving ends of 4-EPB 5049 and 4-DD 4002 may also be compared. Two of the more enduring features of the double-decker units perpetuated on the EPBs were electro-pneumatic brakes and roller-blind headcode panels. Although unsuccessful as a concept, the 4-DD units remained in traffic until October 1971, latterly only operating at the shoulders of the peaks where their slower loading and unloading (the main drawback) wouldn't cause a problem. *Both: John H. Bird/www.anistr.com*

Opposite: The first thirty-six 4-CIG and eighteen 4-BIG units were built at York Works in 1946-66 to replace the PUL and PAN stock on Central Division main-line services and were therefore known as 'Brighton Replacement Stock'. In March 1967 4-CIG 7307 leads a 12-car CIG+BIG+CIG formation forming an Ore – Victoria service on the approach to Clapham Junction. On this date New Wandsworth freight yard at the top of the cutting was still in operation. *Brian Stephenson*

By the summer of 1969 the original green livery had been replaced by British Rail blue and grey and the freight yard had closed but otherwise little has changed. In dappled late-afternoon light, 4-CIG 7307 is again heading for Clapham Junction with an up express from Ore to Victoria. *Brian Stephenson*

Following delivery from York Works but prior to entering service, new 'Brighton Replacement Stock' 4-BIG buffet-car unit 7034 is at the end of a line of similar units parked in a siding west of Ford on 30 August 1965. These were the last Southern electric units to be delivered in green and the yellow warning panel was nicely set off by orange horizontal handrails on either side. *John H. Bird/www.anistr.com*

By 1968 the green paintwork on 4-BIG 7034 now looks rather tired and suffering from the effects of carriage washing chemicals as it leads a Victoria – Ore express passing Coulsdon North on the Quarry line. The unit behind has already been repainted in blue and grey. *Chris Wilson Collection*

This busy scene at Basingstoke was probably captured in the summer of 1967, full electric services on the Bournemouth line having commenced on 10 July. On the left, a maroon liveried Western Region 'Warship' class diesel hydraulic D812 'The Royal Naval Reserve 1859-1959' is in charge of a service from Exeter and Salisbury, while on the right 4-TC trailer unit 403 leads a Bournemouth – Waterloo (headcode '92') semi-fast train. Other points of interest include the redundant water column and, on the far right, one of the S.R. 3-H diesel-electric units with a Reading service.
Chris Wilson Collection

Four years later, blue 'Warship' D818 'Glory' stands at Basingstoke in charge of the 07.15 Exeter St David's – Waterloo service on 25 August 1971, contrasting with the unique 8-VAB unit 8001 calling with another Waterloo-bound service from Bournemouth. ***Bernard Mills***

Kent Coast Electrics – Inside and Out

Above: Six new express four-coach units, based on B.R. standard coach designs and equipped with electro-pneumatic brakes, were turned out from Eastleigh Works in 1956-57 as prototypes of the stock intended for the Kent Coast electrification. Classified 4-CEP and 4-BEP (with buffet) they were similar in concept and layout to the pre-war COR and BUF stock. Following tests, they started their working life on the Central Section and remained there throughout the period covered by this book. Here three of the prototype CEPs, led by unit 7103, pass Wandsworth Common with the 09.28 Victoria – Brighton semi-fast service on 5 August 1956, eight weeks after entering service. *R. C. Riley/The Transport Treasury*

Opposite lower: This most unusual view of half of 4-CEP 7104 was taken at Peckham Rye, where the units were first based for electrical maintenance, on 28 February 1957. The overhaul shed here was only three coaches long, so any longer unit had to be split and shunted before entering. The nearest vehicle is the side-corridor trailer second, virtually identical to equivalent hauled stock. Note that there were no intermediate buffers between vehicles, loads being taken by the buckeye coupler and rubbing-plate. Externally, these units differed in detail from the production Kent Coast stock, principally in design of the windows which were mounted from inside and had no heavy external frames.
R. C. Riley/The Transport Treasury

Below: The interior of a Motor Brake Second from unit 7101 illustrates a second-class open saloon. The aluminium luggage racks are a new innovation but the seating with its wooden ends is little different to the PUL and PAN stock built two decades previously. **David Brown Collection**

The internal appointments of the 1956 prototype 4 CEPs and BEPs were identical to those of contemporary locomotive-hauled stock, then also being built at Eastleigh. The comfortable but outdated design harks back to the 1930s in such features as the string luggage racks and 'tulip' lampshades. This is the official view of a second-class compartment in prototype unit 7101. The 'scarlet boomerang' upholstery was ubiquitous on the S.R. at the time but did not prove to wear well. **S.R. Official/David Brown Collection**

Unit 7105, the first production 4-CEP for the Kent Coast electrification, poses for its official portrait session outside Eastleigh Works when brand new in August 1958. Some external design changes had taken place in line with similar developments to locomotive hauled coaches; in particular the widows were now fitted from outside and had narrow raised frames. Electrically, they were equipped with 1957-type camshaft control gear.
S.R. Official/David Brown Collection

4-CEP unit 7127 has just passed Chart Leacon Works and approaches Ashford leading a 12-coach Victoria – Folkestone Harbour boat train, routed out of London via the Catford loop, on 27 September 1963. Chart Leacon was established as a major maintenance and overhaul facility for Kent Coast and other S.R. electric stock at this time. *Denis Ovenden/Colour Rail*

The newly-formed B.R. Design Panel had some input on the appearance of the interiors in production 4-CEP units, and the centre-gangway open saloon interiors of the motor coaches certainly looked more modern, with much use of plastic laminate panelling and less fussy detailing. Upholstery was the ubiquitous 'Trojan' grey-based pattern, which would spread into most S.R. electric stock in the succeeding twenty years. *S.R. Official/David Brown Collection*

Opposite left: The first class compartments of the 4-CEP and 4-BEPs were extremely comfortable and had all the appointments expected by well-heeled commuters of the period, including intermediate arm-rests, separate seat cushions and extra legroom This official view shows one of the compartments from the trailer composite of unit 7105.
S.R. Official/David Brown Collection

Opposite right: In comparison with the saloons, the second-class compartments of production 4-CEP and 4-BEP stock seemed dull and uninviting, particularly with the wall of boring unrelieved plain grey upholstery. *S.R. Official/David Brown Collection*

47

Opposite: A pair of B.R.-standard '2-HAP' units, with 6067 leading, approach Ashford on 27 September 1963 with a Victoria – Margate stopping service via Maidstone East and Canterbury West. The line of cattle wagons makes an interesting backdrop. *Denis Ovenden/Colour Rail*

B.R. standard-type 2-HAP unit 6005 stands outside Eastleigh Carriage Works when just outshopped in November 1957. Driving trailer composite 77119 is leading. From the left behind the cab, internal arrangements in this vehicle comprised three first class compartments connected by a short side-corridor, a pair of toilets with access from the first and second class sections respectively, and finally a six bay second class open saloon. The first class compartments were of the same length as the seconds, but the larger seat cushions made legroom very cramped.
S.R. Official/David Brown Collection

Tunnel Vision

Opposite: 4-BEP 7011 emerges from the eastern portal of Saltwood tunnel, to the east of Sandling, leading a Charing Cross – Dover Priory service in the summer of 1962, shortly after inauguration of phase 2 of the Kent Coast electrification. It was not common to see a BEP at the front of a train, and photographs of them are therefore quite scarce.
H. Patterson-Rutherford/ Alex Dasi-Sutton Collection

'Nelson' stock worked regularly on the Brighton main line throughout its life. On a sunny day in about 1960, unit 3106 leads a well-filled Victoria – Brighton semi-fast service out of Merstham tunnel on the Quarry line, avoiding Redhill. The gangways on the ends of these units at speed generated much clanking and banging.
Chris Wilson Collection

Looking very smart following a recent repaint, augmented 4-SUB 4580 emerges into the daylight at Woolwich forming a Charing Cross – Dartford via Greenwich service on 17 August 1952. Pre-war units such as this generally carried letter headcodes, in this case 'V' with a bar above, until the ends of their lives. Following withdrawal in March 1954, the wooden bodywork of S.E.R. origin would be consigned to the Newhaven bonfires, but the underframes and bogies would be refurbished for use under new 4-EPB vehicles. *Alan A. Jackson/Chris Wilson Collection*

Opposite: Unit 2921, the very first 4-LAV for the Brighton electrification and delivered from Eastleigh in 1931, speeds away from Redhill tunnel on the Quarry line (avoiding Redhill) with the 15.30 London Bridge – Brighton semi-fast service on 9 April 1964. The LAVs had most of their seating in closed compartments and only one vehicle had a side-corridor and toilets. By this time, they were clearly outdated and subject to much passenger complaint, particularly from Brighton line season-ticket holders. *R.C.T.S. Photographic Archive*

Opposite: 'Sheba' 4-SUB 4107 emerges from Paxton Tunnel and approaches Crystal Palace High Level with a service from Blackfriars on 18 September 1954. The units' famous high seating capacity would not be needed on this moribund branch line from Nunhead which would cease to operate eleven days later, the first S.R. electrified route to be closed.
Rail Archive Stephenson

5-BEL units 3051 and 3053 pass through the deep cutting south of Clayton tunnel between Hassocks and Preston Park with the 14.00 down 'Brighton Belle' from Victoria on New Year's Day 1969. This was the last year the units would be in traditional Pullman livery, already slightly spoiled by the obligatory yellow warning panel.
John H. Bird/www.anistr.com

Opposite: 'Hornby' Co-Co electric locomotive 20003 emerges from Merstham tunnel with the 09.15 Victoria – Newhaven Harbour boat train on 17 September 1966. Entering service in 1948, this locomotive had a different cab design to the earlier pair, somewhat resembling the all-steel 4-SUB units contemporary with it. By this time 20003 had received its final major overhaul and its cabs were equipped with roller-blind headcode panels. *Patrick Russell/Rail Archive Stephenson*

6-COR unit 3049 emerges from Penge tunnel and approaches Penge East station leading a Stewarts Lane – Ramsgate crew training working in March 1967. The ten 6-CORs had been reformed from redundant 6-PUL and PAN units in 1965-66 as short-term Central Division spares but were used on some Kent Coast services during the summers of 1967 and 1968. Their age and poor performance did not endear them to either passengers or staff and all were out of service by mid-November 1968. *Brian Stephenson*

Opposite: Hybrid 4-EPB unit 5262, formed with B.R. standard-type motor coaches from disbanded 2-EPBs and spare S.R.-type trailers, brakes for the Penge East stop with a Victoria – Orpington service, also in March 1967. Although superficially similar, electric suburban vehicles of S.R. and B.R. design differed in almost every detail, and the non-matching coach profiles will be noted.
Brian Stephenson

With the home signal pulled off, 2-BIL unit 2017 approaches Falmer with a lunchtime Hastings – Brighton service on 19 March 1967. Lengthy stopping train duties such as this were exactly what the homely and comfortable BILs, with side corridors and toilets in both coaches, were intended for. *Brian Stephenson*

Left: 4-SUB 4376 has just emerged from Knight's Hill tunnel and runs into Tulse Hill with the 17.52 London Bridge – Epsom Downs service on 5 June 1955, the final day of the long-running and damaging railway strike that year. 4376 was one of relatively few all-compartment SUBs built post-war with steel bodies and was also unusual in having grab rails only around the offside windscreen. The eight-car stop sign, seemingly hanging from a platform light fitting, is another interesting detail.
R. C. Riley/The Transport Library

Opposite: Surrounded by snow and frozen mud, Type JA Electro-Diesel E6002 is in charge of an engineer's or breakdown train at Murston sidings, Sittingbourne, on 20 February 1965. The 600hp diesel installed in these locomotives made them ideal for working into out-of-the-way locations such as this. It is likely a member of the train crew braved the elements to take this photograph.
Chris Wilson Collection

Snow Worries

Opposite: Type HB electro-diesel E6105, rebuilt from surplus Kent Coast type HA 'booster' electric locomotive E5019 at Crewe, speeds through a wintry Eastleigh in charge of a Waterloo – Southampton Docks boat train on 3 February 1969. The locomotive is equipped with non-standard roller blinds with black-on-white numbers, presumably as an experiment. *John H. Bird/www.anistr.com*

4-COR 3109 and 4-BUF 3073 approach journey's end as they snake into Waterloo with a semi-fast service from Portsmouth Harbour on a snowy Saturday 29 November 1969. The power signal box at Waterloo dates from 1936 when the area was re-signalled, and tracks rearranged in preparation for the Portsmouth electrification and the new suburban branch to Chessington. ***Chris Wilson Collection***

4-VEP 7780, in original glossy blue livery with full yellow ends and aluminium double arrows, leaves Waterloo with an Alton service, also on 29 November 1969. The unpainted aluminium window frames were a distinctive feature of these units, which were built in 1968-70 to replace the pre-war LAV, BIL and HAL stock. Also present are 4-SUB 4356 on a Dorking train, 4-VEP 7704 and an unidentified W.R. 'Warship' diesel on a Salisbury and Exeter service. The fact that the Alton and Dorking services were unusually departing from the Windsor lines platforms suggests that engineering work was taking place that day, which can't have been pleasant for the staff on the ground in these conditions. *Both: Chris Wilson Collection*

All-steel 'Tin' 2-HAL 2698, by now in blue livery, approaches Anerley on the fast line with an up main line train bound for London Bridge on a snowy day in January 1969. The service is not identifiable, but it isn't clear whether the headcode panel is obscured by compacted snow or has just fallen-off, a not infrequent occurrence. 2698 survived in traffic until the last day of BIL and HAL operation in July 1971. *Brian Stephenson*

Opposite: Following a heavy snowfall on 11 January 1962, S.R.-type 4-EPB 5043 enters Charing Cross with a Mid-Kent line service from Hayes. In these conditions there will be plenty of steam emanating from the coach interiors when the doors are flung open. At least today the icy platforms make it unlikely anyone will be foolish enough to alight from the train until it has drawn to a halt. *Chris Wilson Collection*

Unidentifiable owing to a sprinkling of sleet (and possibly dirt too) obscuring its unit number, one of the first B.R. standard 4-EPBs in the 53xx number series departs from London Bridge in wintry conditions with a Cannon Street – Sevenoaks service, also on 11 January 1962. Generally similar to the 57xx series 2-EPBs introduced eight years earlier, the seventy units of this class were built at Eastleigh in 1961-63, mainly to replace the 43xx series of 4-SUBs dating from 1925. *Chris Wilson Collection*

Opposite: On a wintry day in January 1969, 4-SUB 4705 departs from Wandsworth Common for Victoria with a service from Beckenham Junction. The superb lighting accentuates the profile of the welded steel 'six-a-side' bodywork of these units. By this time a significant number of 4-SUBs were in the standard glossy blue livery with full yellow ends as seen here. *Brian Stephenson*

Approaching Wandsworth Common station from the opposite direction, 5-BEL 3052 is also beautifully lit as she leads 3053 with the 11.00 down 'Brighton Belle' service on the same date. 3052 has just been outshopped in the lined Pullman version of B.R. blue and grey adopted by the Southern Region for both the 'Belle' and the 'Golden Arrow', but for the time being retains her stencil headcode panel. 3053 is still in traditional umber and cream but will emerge in the new livery the following May. *Brian Stephenson*

A pair of 2-HALs, with 2669 leading, passes Balham with a Victoria – Brighton semi-fast via Redhill in December 1962, its roof having gathered a thick layer of snow from overnight falls. Colour-light signals on curved reinforced concrete posts were a distinctive feature of the Central Section London-area re-signalling scheme of the early 1950s, the section from Battersea Park through Balham to Selhurst being brought into service in October 1952.
Brian Stephenson

Waiting passengers are no doubt relieved to see 4-SUB 4738 pulling into Crystal Palace with a Victoria – Beckenham Junction service in January 1969. Still carrying the now obsolete pre-1967 green livery with a small warning panel, it is evenly illuminated by sunlight reflected off the snow on the opposite platform. Like all production all-steel 4-SUBs from 4621 upwards, the three new saloon vehicles were built using the reclaimed bogies and underframes of pre-war suburban stock, in this case from 1925 Eastern Section units as evidenced by the kinked guard-irons in front of the leading driving wheels.
Brian Stephenson

Passing the Box

4-LAV 2929 calls at the new Gatwick Airport station with the 15.47 Victoria – Brighton stopping service on 30 August 1958. Reconstructed from the former closed racecourse station that year to serve the newly relocated and expanded airport, the existing signal box located on the central island platform 3-4 remained. *J. H. Aston*

Parked underneath the elevated S.E.R. signal box at Orpington, S.R-type 4-EPB 5153 is passed by Maunsell's Schools Class 4-4-0 30929 'Malvern' in charge of an up Kent coast express formed of Bulleid coaches on 2 July 1960. Other EPB and SUB units are berthed in surrounding sidings. Two years later, Phase 2 of the Kent Coast electrification would see the end of steam working on the South Eastern main line and 'Malvern' would be withdrawn.
Dr Terry Gough/The Transport Library

Green-liveried 4-BIG buffet unit 7033 departs from Victoria, emerges from underneath the B.O.A.C. Air Terminal and passes the 1939 Central side signal box with a Victoria – Brighton non-stop service on 5 June 1966. The CIGs and BIGs had totally replaced the 6-PULs and PANs on Brighton line expresses six weeks previously and, while some would mourn the loss of Pullmans on these services, the riding was infinitely calmer and you were far less likely to spill your tea. *Brian Stephenson*

Opposite: 4-SUB 4424 arrives at Charing Cross under the distinctive overhead signal box with a service from Orpington on 9 May 1953. 4424 was augmented from three-car 1579 with new a 'all-steel' trailer in February 1947 and survived until April 1956. Originally dating from 1937, it was one of the last six conversions from existing wooden-bodied steam stock on new underframes, utilising former L.S.W.R. bodywork dating from the turn of the Century. Alone amongst the pre-war suburban stock, 1579-84 (4424-29 after augmentation) were fitted with 1936-type electro-pneumatic control gear, most of which was underframe-mounted and thus freeing up body space for an additional compartment. Photographs of these units are extremely uncommon, the authors knowing of only one other.
Alan A. Jackson/Chris Wilson Collection

Opposite: 4-COR 3105 passes Wimbledon 'B' signal box on the down slow line leading a 12-coach train of 'Nelson' stock in about 1955. The working is not recorded but from the headcode is probably a Bank Holiday rambler's excursion. *Fred Ivey*

South London line 2-car unit 1805 calls at Mitcham with the 12.51 West Croydon – Wimbledon service on Saturday 23 October 1954. These units were frequently seen on this route, particularly in their later years, but this was probably the last day in traffic for 1805.
J. J. Smith/Bluebell Museum Archive

Opposite: Still in green but with recently-applied full yellow ends and hand-painted black unit numbers, 2-BIL 2141 slows for the Esher stop with a Portsmouth/Alton – Waterloo stopping service on an unrecorded date in about 1968. Track has recently been removed from the disused Sandown Park race platform. The semaphore signalling between Surbiton and Woking, including Esher box, lasted until 1970 and the down fast signal is cleared for the next train. *John H. Bird/www.anistr.com*

Bulleid 'Hornby' electric locomotive 20001 passes Glynde in charge of 'The Sussex Venturer' rail tour on Saturday 4 January 1969, en route from Lewes to Hastings via the Polegate – Stone Cross direct line avoiding Eastbourne. This tour, run jointly by the Bulleid Locomotive Preservation Society and the Locomotive Club of Great Britain, was one of the last runs for this locomotive prior to withdrawal. *John H. Bird/www.anistr.com*

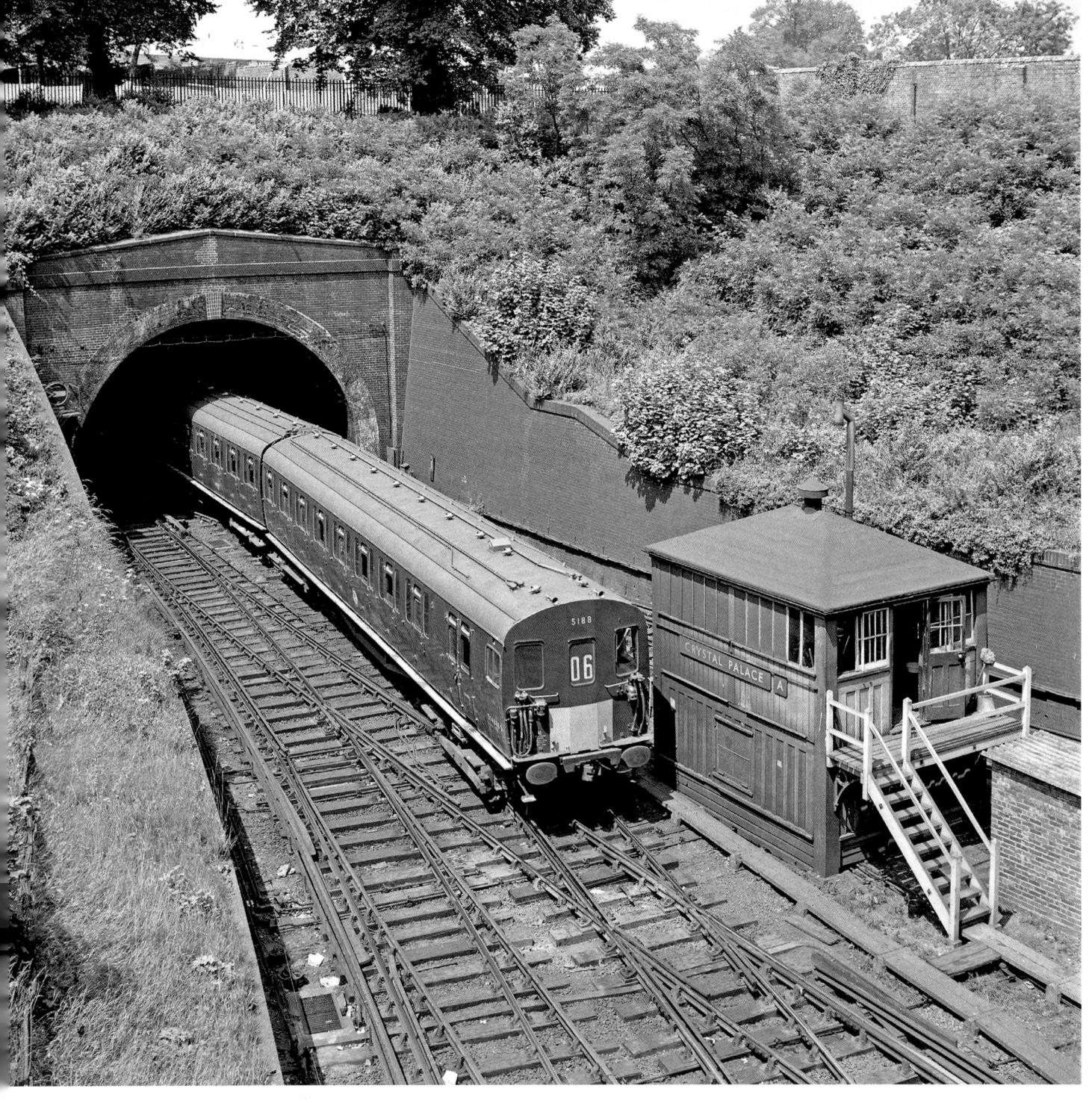

S.R.-type 4-EPB 5188 comes out of Crystal Palace tunnel into the sunshine and passes the antediluvian L.B.S.C.R. 'A' signal box before entering the station with a Victoria – West Croydon service on 5 July 1964. This was one of the EPBs to be given full-length guttering at cantrail height, subtly altering the appearance of the all-steel bodywork. *Brian Stephenson*

Opposite: 6-PAN 3031 leads a 6-PUL negotiating the reverse curve into Lewis with an Eastbourne – London Bridge service in about 1961. Seventeen 6-PANs were built for the 1935 Eastbourne electrification and they generally ran in conjunction with a 6-PUL on Central Section coastal expresses via Haywards Heath. Instead of a Pullman, one of the trailers had a small kitchenette, but catering opportunities were limited and post-war they generally ran closed. The signal box with its impressive array of signals controlled two junctions: between the London and Brighton lines at the station throat, and the Uckfield and Eastbourne/Seaford lines behind the train. **Chris Wilson Collection**

Above: 'Sheba' 4-SUB 4108 approaches Clapham Junction and passes 'B' box with a Victoria – Sutton via Streatham Common and West Croydon service on 5 April 1969. It is still in green livery but now has full yellow ends. These ten prototype 'six-a-side' units with HAL-style domed cab ends and timber roofs were among the first of the second-generation SUBs to disappear, 4108 being withdrawn in May 1972 and subsequently scrapped by Cashmore's at Newport. With their particularly hard and cramped seating, their loss would not be mourned by commuters. *Chris Wilson Collection*

Left: 4-COR 3118 slows for the Petersfield stop and passes the signal box leading a Waterloo – Portsmouth fast service in 1969. The site of the former Midhurst bay platform opposite the box has recently been cleared. *John H. Bird/www.anistr.com*

6-PAN unit 3024 passes Forest Hill leading an evening peak London Bridge – Brighton fast service in August 1964. The post-war 'glasshouse'-style signal box with its rounded elevations was typical of those provided for the early 1950s re-signalling scheme in the area. *Colour Rail*

B.R. standard 2-EPB unit 5739 calls at Waddon Marsh Halt with a Wimbledon – West Croydon service on 21 June 1957. These units replaced the vintage former A.C. stock on this line late in 1954. The power jumper has recently been removed from under the nearside windscreen, and the paintwork around the former mountings has been touched-up. Opened in 1930 with electrification of the line, Waddon Marsh Halt was surrounded by heavy industry, including a gas works and power station. The area was served by an extensive tangle of sidings, amongst which an industrial saddle tank engine could often be seen lurking. The diminutive signal box on the platform also served as a ticket office.
Dr Terry Gough/The Transport Library

Opposite: Bulleid S.R.-type 4-EPB unit 5176 passes New Malden signal box with a Guildford - Waterloo via Cobham service on 8 May 1960. It is running 'wrong line' on the down fast due to bridge renewal work taking place on the up lines; although booked non-stop from Waterloo to Surbiton it is probably crawling as it is hand signalled past the works. 5176 still has early B.R. green livery and its unit number prefixed by 's'. As with unit 5188 already seen, it also has the full-length gutters above the doors.
Dr Terry Gough/The Transport Library

All-steel 4-SUB 4668 enters Waterloo with a service from Horsham in about 1962, passing the 1936 power signal box. 4668 was another 'standard' saloon-type SUB formed from three new coaches using reclaimed underframes and bogies from withdrawn pre-war units, and an existing compartment trailer previously used to augment a pre-war unit from three to four coaches. *Kenneth Field/Rail Archive Stephenson*

Opposite: In original as-built condition, S.R. bodied 4-EPB unit S 5041 runs into Knockholt and passes the distinctive S.E.R. timber signal box with a Charing Cross – Orpington – Sevenoaks service on 5 September 1957. The 'S' (for Southern) prefix to the unit number, seen on several units in this book, was inconsistently applied in the 1948-55 period. The power jumper cable below the driver's windscreen was a feature of early EPBs but was later removed. *Colour Rail*

Everyday Service

Not exactly an everyday working, 6-PUL express unit 3006 picks its way gingerly through the curved platforms at West Norwood leading a diverted Victoria – Brighton non-stop service on 9 March 1965. With its many speed restrictions, the re-routing via Streatham Hill and Norwood Junction for this service today will add several minutes to the usual one-hour timing. Note that there are two motormen in the cab on this occasion. *Brian Stephenson*

Opposite: South London line 2-car unit 1806 stands in Platform 19 at London Bridge, shortly to depart with a lunchtime service for Victoria via Peckham Rye and Denmark Hill on Saturday 21 August 1954. These delightfully quirky units bought photographers out in some numbers as their imminent demise approached, and all had gone by the end of October that year. They were converted in 1928-29 from the motor coaches of the L.B.S.C.R. 1909 A.C. stock built for the line and retained the flattened roof ends above the cabs where the bow collectors had originally been located. Other interesting features included the side-gangway internal arrangements divided into sections by swing-doors, and frosted glass toplights above the quarterlight windows. *Alan A. Jackson/Chris Wilson Collection*

Above: A typical line-up of Southern electric units basks in the sunshine at Waterloo at about midday on Saturday 18 June 1955. On the left, 2-BIL 2071 has not yet had its stencil headcode hooked on but will form a stopping service to Portsmouth & Southsea. In the centre, 2-HAL 2666 prepares to leave with an Alton service, run separately to cater for holiday crowds on the Portsmouth train. On the right, virtually new 4-EPB 5160 will shortly depart with a Guildford via Cobham service, fast to Surbiton.
Alan A. Jackson/Chris Wilson Collection

Right lower: 'Sheba' 4-SUB 4107 runs into the semi-derelict Lordship Lane station with a Blackfriars – Crystal Palace High Level service on 18 September 1954, eleven days before the line closed. Temporary wartime closure, a lack of nearby housing development and the proximity of other stations with a more convenient service all helped to seal the fate of this branch.
Alan A. Jackson/Chris Wilson Collection

Right: South London line 2-car unit 1801 is on home territory as it calls at Denmark Hill with a Victoria – London Bridge via Peckham Rye service on 19 April 1953. Passenger loadings on this line were not high and a single unit was sufficient for much of the day. It is carrying the full-width headcode stencil '2', really intended for the Wimbledon – West Croydon line on which these units also operated; a main line style 2-digit frame, also displaying '2', as seen on page 88, was more usually used on the South London line.
R. C. Riley/The Transport Treasury

Left: 4-SUB 4645 runs into Blackfriars with an evening peak Holborn Viaduct – Orpington service, routed via Herne Hill and Petts Wood, in about 1955. The rather drab atmosphere and surroundings, including the clothes worn by homegoing office workers, are typical of their era. Situated on the north bank of the Thames close to St. Paul's Cathedral, Blackfriars was definitely the least impressive of the S.R.s main London stations with just three terminating bays, situated to the right of the incoming train. *Fred Ivey*

Opposite: The train shown in this picture is not actually electric, although all the coaches previously had been. B.R.C.W. type 3 KA diesel-electric locomotive D6528 hauls set 900 approaching Anerley with the 07.25 Tunbridge Wells West–London Bridge via East Grinstead service on 8 November 1963. Set 900 had been hastily formed in September 1963 from 2-BIL 2006 with five redundant 'six-a-side' suburban trailers inserted to provide an air-braked and electrically heated rake for particular rush hour services on the Oxted line, which had just been dieselised. It was classified 7-TC and renumbered 701 in 1966, but there was never any intention to operate it in push-pull mode. It was withdrawn in 1967, shortly after an overhaul and repaint into blue, but the centre trailers all saw further service in SUB or EPB units. *Brian Stephenson*

L.B.S.C.R.-bodied 4-SUB 4571 calls at London Bridge (Eastern) with a Charing Cross – Dartford via Bexleyheath service during the Saturday lunch-time rush-hour on 11 October 1952. At this time 4571 unusually had two wooden-bodied trailers; upon withdrawal in March 1956 one of these was reformed into unit 4502 and lasted in service until November 1959. *Alan A. Jackson/Chris Wilson Collection*

2-BIL 2018 descends from the slight hump over the River Arun bridge on the approach to Ford, where it will not call, leading a 2-HAL on a Brighton – Portsmouth Harbour semi-fast service in about 1968. *Chris Wilson Collection*

Opposite: 2-HAL unit 2661 stands in platform 4B at Reading General on 8 January 1969, waiting to depart a train to Waterloo via Ascot, where it will attach to a portion from Guildford via Aldershot. This new platform was built in 1965 to replace the adjacent Reading (Southern) station and handled both electric services from Waterloo and the diesel-worked Redhill and Tonbridge line trains. Still green, 2661 has recently gained a full yellow end on which the unit numbers are non-standard. A Western Region Pressed Steel diesel unit, used for Paddington suburban services, vibrates in platform 5. *John H. Bird/www.anistr.com*

Still looking smart in green with a small warning panel even on a filthy rainy day, 2-HAL unit 2650 calls at the typical L.S.W.R. wayside station at Frimley with the 12.48 Waterloo – Guildford via Ascot on a wet 19 May 1969. It will shortly cross the South Western main line and traverse the unusual single line section to Ash Vale Junction. The characteristic flush-fitting quarterlights with rounded corners are clearly visible on these distinctive Bulleid design units. *John H. Bird/www.anistr.com*

Opposite: On an unrecorded date in the summer of 1964, 'booster' electric locomotive 20003 is in charge of the 17.14 Newhaven Harbour – Victoria boat train, seen approaching Clapham Junction from the Boutflower Road bridge. At this stage in its career 20003 retained folding headcode discs and redundant jumper cables for multiple working with later class members which were, sadly, never built. *Brian Stephenson*

A few all-steel SUBs were experimentally fitted with roller-blind headcode panels rather than the clip-on stencils hitherto standard. One such was 4721, seen calling at Whitton with an anti-clockwise Hounslow loop service (headcode '89') on 26 August 1970. It is still in green livery but with the full yellow ends applied from 1967. Whitton station, built for the 1930 Windsor electrification, displays the somewhat utilitarian concrete and steel platform architecture used by the S.R. for new wayside stations at this time. *John Scrace*

Left: Having recently acquired a small yellow warning panel and air horns, the friendly face of 2-BIL 2034 is caught by sunshine at Waterloo before departing with an Alton and Portsmouth & Southsea stopping service in about 1966. From left to right the jumper cables across the front are for control, lighting and power respectively. 2034 was later painted blue in July 1969 and was in service on the final day of BIL and HAL operation, 29 July 1971. *Chris Wilson Collection*

Opposite Top: 4-COR units 3124 and 3148, each temporarily reformed with a former 6-PUL motor coach from withdrawn units 3017 and 3018 respectively, pass Clapham Junction with the 19.17 Waterloo – Farnham service on 16 July 1964. This interesting reformation had occurred the previous month to release two COR-type motor coaches for push-pull trials, and the resulting additional four motors in the eight-car train gave this pair a sprightly performance. The two 'Nelson' units reverted to normal in July 1965. *Brian Stephenson*

Opposite Bottom: 4-COR 3114, another of the exclusive group of units outshopped in blue with small yellow panels, snakes through the reverse curves near Godalming leading a Waterloo – Portsmouth Harbour express in about November 1966. *Chris Wilson Collection*

Opposite: 4-COR 3142 leads two sister units passing Wandsworth Common with a rambler's excursion from Victoria on Sunday 26 May 1963. The cab-front gangway plate tended to oscillate alarmingly from side to side when at speed, giving rise to the term 'belly-wobblers' also applied to this stock. *Brian Stephenson*

2-BIL 2081 stands at Aldershot on 9 September 1969 while reversing on its way from Waterloo to Guildford via Ascot. Reversals en route were rare on Southern electric services, Eastbourne and Littlehampton being the only other examples. *Chris Wilson Collection*

Opposite: Single S.R.-type 2-EPB 5664 on a Waterloo – Weybridge service passes Addlestone Moor on 30 April 1966, another unit for Windsor having divided from it at Staines. Introduced in 1960, these were the last S.R. electric units built with Bulleid-style bodywork on reclaimed 62' underframes and bogies, in this case from scrapped 2-NOL vehicles. They were also the only suburban stock with entirely open saloon accommodation. On their introduction they were classified as 2-NOP in Ian Allan 'ABC' spotting books, but this was never official. *Chris Wilson Collection*

A pair of 2-NOL units, with 1824 nearest, stands at Hastings after arrival with a stopping service from Brighton on 18 June 1958. Introduced in 1934, the NOLs were a two-car version of the standard pre-war suburban units and had bodies rebuilt from L.S.W.R. steam stock dating from around the turn of the Century. Although it still appears to be in excellent external condition, 1824 would be withdrawn the following February and its underframes reused for new EPB stock. *Chris Wilson Collection*

The first Bulleid/Raworth 'Hornby' electric locomotive 20001 is in charge of the 09.15 Victoria - Newhaven Harbour boat train, which has just passed through Clapham Junction on an unrecorded date in the summer of 1964. The train is formed of a mixture of Bulleid and B.R. standard coaches. 20001 is carrying lined bright green livery and will retain folding headcode discs and marker lights until its final overhaul. The overhead electrification plate seems somewhat spurious even though the locomotive carries a pantograph. *Brian Stephenson*

Opposite: 4-CEP 7169 leads a twelve-coach formation between Beckenham Junction and Shortlands with a down Kent Coast service in the summer of 1969. By this time, it was unusual to see an entire train in green, although the second unit has gained a full yellow end. It would not be long before British Rail blue and grey would be universal on Southern Region express stock, and it would remain so throughout the 1970s.
Patrick Russell/Rail Archive Stephenson

4-COR 3138 is seen pulling out of Woking leading a COR+RES+COR formation working a Waterloo - Portsmouth Harbour fast in around 1960. Woking was rebuilt in the 'moderne' style, with extensive use of curved elevations, facing concrete and Crittall steel-framed windows, for the 1937 Portsmouth electrification. Note also the characteristic S.R. 'glasshouse' signal box, and the 'Queen Mary' bogie brake van parked on the up side. *Chris Wilson Collection*

Opposite: Original 1931 vintage 4-LAV unit 2924 is coupled to one of the two 1940 Bulleid-type units as it hums past track relaying work in progress north of East Croydon on an unknown date in about 1968, at a time when high-visibility clothing was not yet de rigeur for gangers. The pair are forming a Brighton – Victoria stopping service and the next stop will be Clapham Junction. *Chris Wilson Collection*

Opposite: Bulleid/Raworth electric locomotive 20003 arrives at Victoria with the morning boat train from Newhaven Harbour on 30 June 1949. This was the very first express passenger service to be hauled by an electric locomotive in Great Britain and the inaugural run had taken place on the previous 15 May, following electrification of the track serving the quayside platform. 20003 carries its original livery of lined Southern Railway malachite green but, being delivered from Eastleigh Works in 1948 following nationalisation, carries 'British Railways' on its sides. The boat train stock for this service, some of S.E.C.R. design dating back to the 1920s, was the first to be painted in the new B.R. carmine and cream ('or blood and custard') livery.
John P. Wilson
Rail Archive Stephenson

By a quirk of history, the Southern Region inherited the Waterloo and City tube line, known to generations of City office workers as 'The Drain'. Promoted by the L.S.W.R. and opening in 1898, it was London's second tube railway and also its shortest, serving just two stations. The original rolling stock, mainly of American origin, was replaced in 1940 by new cars with aluminium bodies, designed by Bulleid and built at Eastleigh. This view shows a train of 1940 stock at Bank on 7 March 1953.
Chris Wilson Collection

2-BIL 2047 departs from Woking and heads down the South Western main line towards Brookwood leading a mixed BIL/HAL formation on the 12.27 Waterloo – Alton service on 13 September 1964. Because the Farnborough Air Show was taking place, served by a bus connection from Aldershot, this service was formed of eight coaches. *Brian Stephenson*

Opposite: Working solo, 6-PUL unit 3003 passes Wandsworth Common forming the 12.00 Victoria – Brighton non-stop service on 28 March 1965. Pullman Composite Car 'Grace' is the third vehicle back. There is plenty of sporting activity taking place on the pitches behind. *Brian Stephenson*

Opposite: By 20 January 1961, the only pre-war 4-SUBs left were augmented 1925 contractor-built units in the 4300-54 series, and these were disappearing rapidly. 4311 was one of the 'short-frame' units built for the Guildford and Dorking electrification and is seen here at Surbiton displaying 'H with bar', indicating a Waterloo – Hampton Court working. These letter headcodes, first introduced by the L.S.W.R. in 1915, would vanish with them. 4311 was withdrawn on 8 April that year and all four vehicles were eventually broken up at Newhaven.
Dr Terry Gough/The Transport Library

2-NOL unit 1816 stands in platform 3 at Hastings on 6 September 1957, having just arrived with a stopping service from Brighton and Eastbourne. Entering service late in 1934 but using L.S.W.R. wooden bodywork then already a third of a century old, 1824 would be withdrawn eighteen months later and its bogies and underframes used under new 2-EPB units for the Windsor line. Passengers travelling towards Ashford on the train at platform 2 would enjoy the comforts of an equally ancient ex-S.E.C.R. 'birdcage' set. *Denis Ovenden/Colour Rail*

When photographed on 12 July 1955, Maze Hill station was in the throes of platform lengthening using pre-cast concrete components as part of the 'ten car scheme' to increase capacity on South Eastern suburban routes out of Charing Cross and Cannon St. Together with power supply renewal and upgrade, and additional rolling stock, this work constituted a capital investment comparable to the original electrification schemes of the 1920s. 4-EPB 5113 calls with a Dartford – Cannon Street via Greenwich working. It is still in original condition with an 'S' prefix to its number and unit-end power jumpers. Like Blackheath on page 138, Maze Hill carriage sidings played host to spare stock, some of considerable vintage, which lay idle most of the year. *Alan A. Jackson/Chris Wilson Collection*

4-SUB 4622 draws out of West Norwood with a Victoria – Coulsdon North service on 9 March 1965, diverted via Streatham Hill and Crystal Palace due to engineering work on the main line. 4622 also had recycled underframes and bogies from pre-war stock and the leading bogie is of the 'central' type with straight guard-irons in front of the leading wheels. At this time there were still many units without yellow warning panels as the Southern was slower than the other regions in adopting these on their units and locomotives. *Brian Stephenson*

2-BIL unit 2101 curves onto the Guildford line at Woking Junction, leading a sister unit with the 12.27 Waterloo – Portsmouth & Southsea working on 13 September 1964. Behind the train is one of the typical mercury-arc rectifier substations provided for the 1937 Portsmouth electrification scheme. There were unfulfilled plans to provide a flying junction at this congested location. *Brian Stephenson*

Seen from the Boutflower Road bridge another pair of 4-LAV units, led by 2937, accelerates away from Clapham Junction with a Victoria – Brighton stopping service on 15 May 1964. Spending their time continuously shuttling up and down the Brighton line, the LAV units accumulated very high mileages during their 35-year lifespans. Unit 2937 was withdrawn in June 1968 and scrapped by Steel Breaking at Chesterfield. *Brian Stephenson*

Opposite: This busy scene at Brighton station dates from about 1962. In the centre, 4-LAV unit 2932 is just pulling out with a Victoria via Redhill semi-fast service. Opposite, a Pullman Car with her cosy armchairs and tablecloths waits invitingly as passengers walk up the platform to board a 6-PUL unit forming the following non-stop service to the capital. On the far left, a van train is being loaded with a varied selection of goods and parcels.
Kenneth Field
Rail Archive
Stephenson

On 28 October 1962 work was underway to replace the 1900 steel skew bridge carrying the Quarry line over the original 1839 Redhill line at Hooley, between Coulsdon South and Merstham, with a new reinforced concrete structure. In those days' efforts were made to keep the train service running during engineering works of this kind, and 4-LAV 2942 is proceeding past with a Victoria – Brighton stopping service, presumably at a crawl. How times change!
Chris Wilson Collection

2-BIL 2117 approaches Hove with a Brighton – Portsmouth Harbour semi-fast service on 12 March 1967. The lines on the left are the Cliftonville curve from Preston Park, used by trains from London to Hove and beyond avoiding Brighton. *Brian Stephenson*

Opposite: 2-EPB 5791 departs from Victoria with a South London line service to London Bridge via Peckham Rye on an unrecorded date in 1964. Unit 5791 was a former 'Tyneside' unit built at Eastleigh and transferred to the S.R. after the Newcastle – South Shields line was de-electrified the previous year. These units could easily be recognised by their shallow headcode panels and extra-long brake vans. This view is taken from a passing 4-SUB unit and the B.O.A.C. Air Terminal, originally built by Imperial Airways before the war, dominates the skyline. *Chris Wilson Collection*

The final 2-BIL unit 2152, built in 1938 for the Reading line electrification, is on home territory as it approaches Virginia Water leading a Waterloo – Reading Southern service on 2 May 1965. At Ascot the rear unit will uncouple and run to Guildford via Aldershot. *Brian Stephenson*

In excellent late spring evening light, 4-COR 3137 leads a COR+BUF+COR formation through Clapham cutting with the 18.14 Waterloo – Portsmouth Harbour fast service on 15 May 1964. The BUF units had been transferred from the Mid-Sussex line to the Portsmouth direct line the previous January. *Brian Stephenson*

4210 was one of the original L.S.W.R. bullet-nosed 'nutcracker' suburban units dating from the 1915-16 electrification, later lengthened on new underframes and then augmented to four coaches with another similar vehicle to become a 4-SUB, On 11 March 1953 it formed the 11.40 Victoria – West Croydon service, and is passing over the junction north of West Norwood. The line on the right went to Tulse Hill. Close observation of the third coach reveals a large window, indicating the position of a small 'saloon' with some longitudinal seating, originally first class. 4210 was withdrawn in October 1955, after which its wooden bodywork was scrapped at Longhedge and its underframes and bogies reused under new 4-EPB vehicles.
R. C. Riley/The Transport Treasury

Still without yellow warning panels at this late date, 2-HAL unit 2653 departs from Hove with a Littlehampton – Brighton service on 12 March 1967. A type HA 'booster' electric locomotive, with its pantograph removed, waits in an adjacent siding for its next duty. *Brian Stephenson*

Like Woking, Surbiton station was reconstructed in the brick and concrete 'moderne' style to the designs of S.R. architect James Robb-Scott in 1937 at the time of the Portsmouth No.1 electrification. The covered footbridge, luggage lift and clock-tower above the main station entrance were clearly influenced by Charles Holden's designs for the London Underground, which Robb-Scott could arguably never quite match. 4-COR 3132 speeds through leading a Waterloo – Portsmouth Harbour fast service in about 1962. *Colour-Rail*

6-PUL 3013, including Pullman Composite Car 'Brenda', passes under the A3 Battersea Rise road bridge and sweeps around the curve on the approach to Clapham Junction leading a 6-PAN with a Brighton – Victoria non-stop service in about 1964. 6-PUL + 6-PAN was the standard formation for Central Section coastal expresses via Haywards Heath but the lack of a through gangway between units meant that passengers expecting on-board refreshments would need to be travelling in the PUL. *Brian Stephenson*

Surrounded by evidence of the 'blitz', augmented 4-SUB 4551 approaches Holborn Viaduct with a 'roundabout' service from Victoria via Streatham Hill, West Croydon, Sutton, Wimbledon and Tulse Hill on 1 May 1954. The former Ludgate Hill station in the background, closed in 1929 and never served by electric trains, remains remarkably intact. 4551 was formed from lengthened L.B.S.C.R. A.C. overhead vehicles. It was reformed in November 1956 when its steel augmentation trailer went to a new 4-EPB and was replaced by another 'Brighton' coach. Renumbered 4511, it then survived in service as late as 2 January 1960, being one the three very last wooden-bodied 4-SUBs. *R. C. Riley/The Transport Treasury*

A pair of 4-LAV units led by 2938 departs from Clapham Junction with an afternoon Victoria – Brighton stopping service on 21 May 1965. The flattened brake van sides were copied from contemporary Maunsell steam stock but gave the cab front a rather starved appearance and were not repeated on later units. The U.I.C. yellow cantrail bands indicate the odd arrangement of first-class compartments, as three in the non-corridor trailer were downclassed in the 1950s, leaving just two. *Brian Stephenson*

Opposite: 6-PAN 3028 approaches Clapham Junction leading a Brighton – Victoria non-stop service in 1964. With their smooth cab ends and 'airstream' sliding window ventilators. the all-steel motor coaches of these units are considered among the most handsome of Southern electric vehicles. 3028 was withdrawn in October 1965; the three 'normal' corridor trailers then went into 6-COR 3048 and the motor coaches and pantry car were scrapped by King's of Wymondham in 1966. *Brian Stephenson*

Electric trains only travelled over the old Swale bridge for about nine months, and photographs are therefore very rare. S.R.-type 2-HAP 5615 crosses the 'old' Swale lifting bridge From the Isle of Sheppey onto the mainland leading a B.R. type unit with a Sheerness – Sittingbourne shuttle on 9 April 1960. The distinctive toilet window of the driving trailer is the same as on Bulleid steam stock built nearly a decade earlier.
J. J. Smith/Bluebell Railway Archive

4-SUB units did occasionally reach the south coast on scheduled passenger services coupled to LAV, NOL, BIL or HAL stock and were also regularly used for summer and bank holiday extras. However, in this view 4699 is seen passing Fishersgate Halt in December 1967 with a Christmas mail train, another use to which they were regularly put. 4699 was another of the small number of SUBs experimentally equipped with roller-blind headcode panels of various types, in this case flush with the cab front. Avoiding the need to be changed externally and with no danger of them dropping off onto the track, they became a standard fitting on new S.R. electric stock from the 4 EPBs onwards. Fishersgate Halt (the suffix was lost in 1969) was opened as a railmotor halt in 1905 but not equipped with the basic ticket office shed seen to the right until electrification in 1933. ***Chris Wilson Collection***

While 4-LAV units were occasionally diagrammed off their Brighton main line haunts with the odd coastal duty to Eastbourne, Hastings or Portsmouth, it was rare to see them on suburban duties. On a most unusual working and substituting for a 4-SUB, 2930 calls at Epsom with a Guildford – London Bridge service (headcode 03) on a wet 5 December 1967. The photographer lived in Ashtead (the previous station) and probably could not believe his luck when this pulled in. No doubt a quick dash through the subway was undertaken to obtain this view.
Alan A. Jackson/Chris Wilson Collection

Opposite: Engineering work was taking place at New Malden on Sunday 8 May 1960, the 'wrecking ball' on a chain suggesting demolition of remaining buildings on the disused central island platform. The up lines were closed but services continued to run with up trains being rerouted over the down fast line. A pair of 2-BIL units, with 2086 leading, passes the signalbox on their way from Portsmouth and Alton with a stopping service to Waterloo, having combined at Woking.
Dr Terry Gough
The Transport Library

Augmented 4-SUB s4190 calls at London Bridge (Eastern) with a Charing Cross-Sevenoaks train on 17 July 1949. Typical of the electric units provided for the suburban electrification schemes of the 1920s, this unit had L.S.W.R. steam-stock bodywork on new underframes. It was lengthened from three to four coaches with a similar coach from a former trailer set in 1948. Livery is Southern Railway post-war malachite green with 'sunshine' lettering, but 'British Railways' has been added to the van sides. 4190 survived in service until January 1956 and was broken up at Newhaven, its underframes and bogies being refurbished for use under new all-steel 4-EPB vehicles.
Bluebell Museum Archive

Another former L.S.W.R. 'nutcracker' 4-SUB 4210, dating from the original South Western suburban electrification and later rebuilt on new underframes before being lengthened to four coaches with an ex-trailer set vehicle in January 1947, departs from Blackheath with a Bexleyheath line service to Charing Cross on 12 March 1955, only seven months before its demise the following October. The sidings on the left hold an assortment of steam stock used for summer-dated extras; the rake nearest the camera comprises mainly S.E.C.R. 100-seater compartment thirds, which had originally been built with conversion to EMU vehicles in mind but were never used as such. In 1968 these same sidings would hold withdrawn 4-LAV units.
Alan A. Jackson/Chris Wilson Collection

Opposite: 2-BIL 2007 was one of the ten pre-production units built at Eastleigh in 1934 and financed from the Eastbourne electrification scheme. They differed in many details from the production units numbered from 2011 upwards; among the obvious features are the ventilator bonnets above the door droplights and a full seven compartments (rather than six and a 'half-compartment') in the motor coach. Both these features are visible in this view of 2007 calling at Goring-by-Sea with a Brighton – Portsmouth Harbour stopping service in 1967. These early BILs were among the first to be withdrawn, 2007 being taken out of service in July 1968 and later scrapped by Bird's at Long Marston.
John Vaughan/Chris Wilson Collection

Still looking smart after twenty-five years in service, unit 2132 leads an eight-coach train of 2-BILs heading away from Clapham Junction with the 12.27 Waterloo – Alton and Portsmouth stopping service on 1 June 1963. First stop will be at Surbiton and the train will divide at Woking. 2132 was one of the Reading line BILs dating from 1938, and detail differences included thicker 'Alpax' alloy window frames and Spencer-Moulton self-contained buffers as fitted to the express stock. *Brian Stephenson*

The driver chats to a bystander as augmented 4-SUB 4329 calls at Wimbledon platform 5 with an anti-clockwise Kingston 'roundabout' service to Waterloo on 16 February 1961. This was one of the 1925 units for the Eastern Section which had longer underframes and flatter fronts than the Western Section units. 4329 had the distinction of being the last pre-war suburban unit to survive, last running in traffic on Friday 12 January 1962. In the background a train of London Transport District Line 'Q stock', with its quirky mixture of older clerestory-roofed and newer flared-bottomed cars, will shortly depart from platform 1 for Earl's Court and beyond, travelling over B.R.-owned lines as far as East Putney.
Dr Terry Gough/The Transport Library

Side by Side

The lack of a conductor rail indicates that our first side by side view is off the electrified network and was taken at Fareham in November 1965. On the left, type JA electro-diesel E6006 is using its 600hp diesel capability to propel a test train. To its right, one of the smart new Swindon 'Inter-City' D.M.U.s operated by the Western Region calls with a Portsmouth Harbour – Cardiff General service. The yellow gangway cover, a feature of these units, is already rather grubby but E6006 is yet to receive any sort of warning panel. *John H. Bird/www.anistr.com*

This view of the east side of Brighton station dates from 1968. Dominating the scene is green-liveried 2-BIL unit 2023, about to depart from platform 8 with an Eastbourne and Ore service. Standing in platform 9 is an unidentified B.R.C.W. type 3 of the KB subclass with narrow body to fit the Tonbridge – Hastings line, in charge of a service to Victoria via Uckfield and Oxted. *John Vaughan/Chris Wilson Collection*

S.R.-bodied 2-HAP 5604 has just arrived at Maidstone West with a terminating service from Charing Cross, which would have split off a portion for Gillingham at Strood, on 6 April 1960. Passing on the centre road is 33033, one of Bulleid's ugly duckling 'Q1' 0-6-0 tender locomotives with a freight, probably bound for Tonbridge Yard. It would be another two years until the line south to Paddock Wood along the Medway valley would be electrified.
Dr Terry Gough
The Transport Library

Opposite: Three 4-COR units, 3126, 3166 and 3125, line up at London Bridge with evening rush-hour services to the Sussex coast on an unrecorded date in 1969. Headcode 17 shows that 3125 is heading for Worthing and Littlehampton, and the other two are on Brighton and Eastbourne services. These were among the last regular workings for 'Nelson' stock on the Brighton main line.
John Day Collection
Rail Photoprints

On the original 1839 London and Croydon Railway route, Norwood Junction-based 'E2' 0-6-0T steam loco 32104 gives added push to a heavy freight about to ascend Brockley bank with a New Cross Gate – East Croydon trip working on Saturday 7 September 1957. To its right, all-steel 4-SUB 4752 approaches Brockley station with a London Bridge 'roundabout' service. *J. J. Smith/Bluebell Museum Archive*

Two pre-war suburban units, both augmented to 4-SUB post-war with a new 'six-a-side' trailer, pass at Clapham Junction in about 1955. On the right, 1925-built 'short-frame' unit 4309 unusually displays numerical headcode '8' and is probably forming a holiday extra to the south coast. Unit 4558 on the left was converted from L.B.S.C.R. A.C. 'overhead' vehicles and is on a Victoria-bound service. 4558 was reformed as 4517 in January 1957 and finally withdrawn at the end of October 1959, being amongst the last wooden-bodied units to go, and 4309 lasted only six months longer. In both cases their fate was the scrap sidings at Newhaven. The large running-in board on the right dates from the pre-grouping era. *David Brown Collection*

Wooden-bodied pre-1939 suburban units occupy platforms 4 and 5 at Charing Cross on 6 October 1951, both by now augmented to 4-SUB with a new 'six-a-side steel trailer. On the left, S.E.C.R.-bodied 4580 (originally three-coach 1620) is on a service to Hayes via Lewisham (headcode 'H'), while on the right L.B.S.C.R.-bodied 4561 (previously 1766) is bound for Orpington and Sevenoaks (inverted 'V'). Note the different unit number styles. *John H. Meredith*

Opposite: 4-CORs 3142 and 3168 on Waterloo services flank class 45 'Peak' 69 on a summer Saturday inter-regional at Portsmouth Harbour on 23 August 1969. These massive 2000hp 1Co-Co1 diesels were an unusual sight on the south coast
John H. Bird/www.anistr.com

This busy morning rush-hour scene on the South Western main line approach to Clapham Junction was recorded on 13 July 1964. In the up direction, 4-SUB 4744 and 4-COR 3115 approach on Waterloo-bound services from Shepperton and Woking respectively, while on the far left another SUB heads for the suburbs. By this date yellow warning panels were starting to appear on the S.R., but only the COR has one so far. *Brian Stephenson*

This fascinating juxtaposition of the old and the new was seen at Shepherds Well on 21 April 1960 and makes an interesting contrast with the picture on page 19. 4-CEP unit 7144, then in traffic for less than a year, pulls away towards Canterbury with a Dover Priory – Victoria stopping service. At this time the last vehicle indication was still by traditional tail lamp and the roller blinds at the rear of the train displayed large white blanks. Overhead trolley wires have been erected over the East Kent Light Railway exchange siding to allow the pantograph-equipped type HA E5000 electric locomotives to work on to it with coal trains to and from Tilmanstone Colliery. An S.E.C.R. 'O1' class 0-6-0 waits to go on to the E.K.L.R. with brake van S 55724.
Dr Terry Gough/The Transport Library

Looking towards Waterloo on the former London & South Western Railway's main line through Clapham Cutting on 1 July 1967, a pair of typical electric services approach in the sunshine. On the down fast line to the left, 2-HAL 2682 leads a stopping service to Alton and Portsmouth & Southsea, dividing at Woking. On the down slow 4-SUB 4603, one of a small batch of seven units with saloon motor coaches and two compartment trailers, forms a suburban service to Shepperton. *Brian Stephenson*

Left: West Croydon station, serving the busy North End shopping area, was comprehensively rebuilt in 1929, finally removing the original 1839 London and Croydon Railway's train shed and bay platforms. A south-facing bay was let-in to the country end of the Up platform specifically for the Wimbledon service, electrified in 1930. On Saturday 23 October 1954 two-car unit 1805, whose coaches dated from the 1909 South London line A.C. electrification, waits to depart with the 09.51 to Wimbledon, on possibly its last day in service. On the Down platform, a steel 4-SUB unit forms a Sutton, Wimbledon and Holborn Viaduct service; this was certainly not the quickest way to reach London from Croydon.
J.J. Smith/Bluebell Museum Archive

Top right: Blue-liveried 2-HAL 2610 and 2-BIL 2112 run into Clapham Junction with an afternoon Waterloo – Reading/Guildford service on 22 November 1970, passing Class 09 shunter D4103 which is returning the empty milk tankers from Vauxhall to Clapham Yard.
Gordon Edgar/Rail Photoprints

Bottom right: This typical summer Saturday line-up at Bournemouth dates from 1967. On the left, Western Region Type 3 B-B Diesel Hydraulic 'Hymek' D7057 awaits departure with 1M09 16.29 Poole-Birmingham inter-regional. 3-TC trailer set 301 is at the head of a semi-fast service to Waterloo, probably propelled by an electro-diesel, while 4-VEP electric unit 7710 will follow with a stopping service, also bound for London. **Chris Wilson Collection**

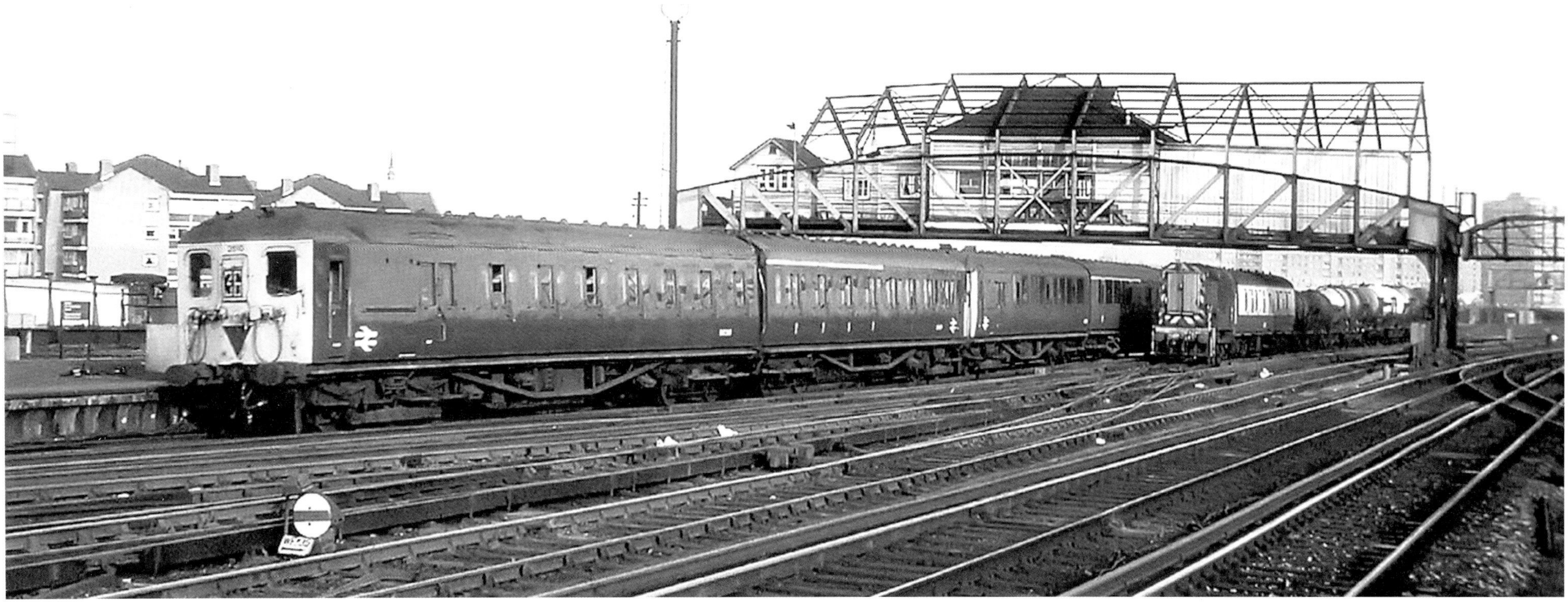

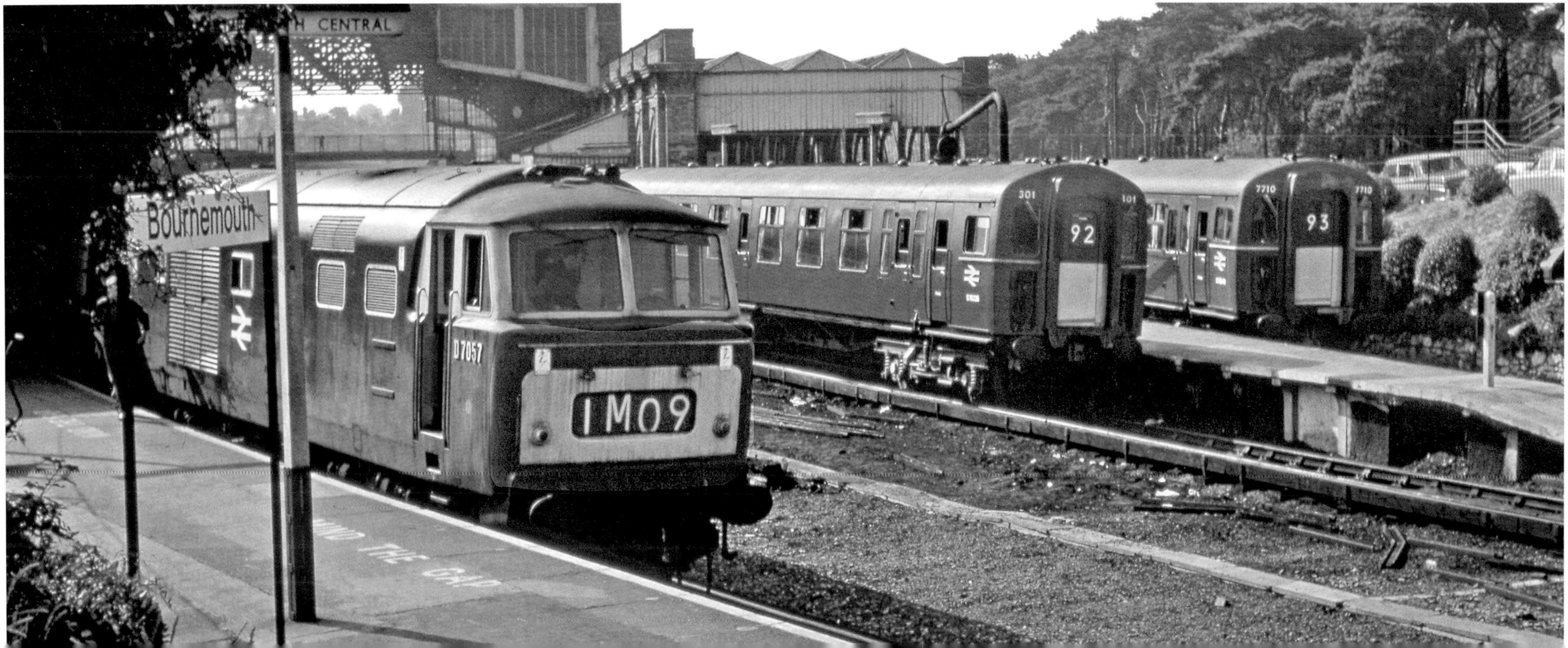

H CENTRAL
Bournemouth
D7057
1M09
301
101
92
7710
7710
93

6-TC 601 was the experimental non-powered unit used to develop and trial the push-pull system as used on the Bournemouth line. It was converted at Eastleigh in the first half of 1965 using redundant 4-COR-type motor coaches and 6-PUL and PAN trailers, and was equipped with electro-pneumatic brakes and the standard post-1951 E.M.U. control system. It is seen here in original condition at Three Bridges in November 1965, during push-pull trials to Littlehampton with the first production type JB electro-diesel E6007. The motor bogies have been replaced by trailer bogies, while the cab ends now have waist-level E.P. brake hoses on both sides, a 27-wire control jumper on the offside and a standard E.T.H. cable.
Duncan Simmons/Strathwood Library Collection

Opposite: To work in push-pull mode with 601, B.R.C.W. KA diesel D6580 was experimentally modified with a control system which converted the four positions of an E.M.U. controller to four diesel engine speeds. Its appearance was significantly altered by the addition of a waist-level 27-wire control jumper and electro-pneumatic brake pipes, and it was given small yellow warning panels. D6580 was rarely photographed, even when working in passenger service with 601 on the Oxted line in 1966-67. In this August 1967 view it is waiting to enter Eastleigh Works to be converted into the last of the 'standard' push-pull locomotives, including tidying up the pipework, fitting buckeye couplers and repainting into blue livery.
Strathwood Library Collection

Towards Push & Pull on the Bournemouth Line

Newly converted push-pull fitted type KA diesel D6520 and an unidentified 4-TC trailer unit stand at Eastleigh, probably on test, in early 1967. Following the experimental conversion of D6580 in 1965 to work in multiple with electric stock, a total of nineteen of the class were fitted with the appropriate equipment for the Bournemouth electrification, principally to power TC units on the non-electrified section between Bournemouth and Weymouth. With their waist-level control jumpers and brake pipes, they inevitably became known as 'bagpipes'. *Chris Wilson Collection*

Opposite: 4-TC 412 trailer unit passes Eastleigh with an unidentified southbound working, possibly on test or crew training, in the spring of 1967. The motive power propelling at the rear is not recorded, but the train appears to have twelve vehicles so would probably have been a 4-REP tractor unit. *John Vaughan/Chris Wilson Collection*

4-TC 404 leads an eleven-coach train propelled by a type JB electro-diesel near Pirbright Junction an up Bournemouth – Waterloo semi-fast service in early June 1967. It has just passed the down 'Bournemouth Belle' and another train of steam stock; the lack of steam suggests both were diesel-hauled. Full electric services on the Bournemouth line, with accelerated and more frequent trains, commenced on Monday 10 June 1967. *Brian Stephenson*

Opposite: Type JB E6041 is at the rear of a formation comprising three 4-TC units, forming a Waterloo – Bournemouth service between Brookwood and Farnborough on 1 June 1967. The 3200hp of two of these locomotives combined would have been equivalent to a 4-REP tractor unit, although possibly not required on this working to steam timings. The two red blocks on the headcode panel, illuminated from behind, indicated to signalmen the rear of the train in place of a tail lamp, while the two small white dots showed an electro-diesel. *Brian Stephenson*

The high bridge carrying Totters Lane over the South Western main line between Hook and Winchfield forms an attractive backdrop as type JB electro-diesel E6037 passes underneath hauling a train of three 4-TC units forming an up Bournemouth line service in May 1967, during the change-over year of steam operation on the Bournemouth-Weymouth expresses. *Brian Stephenson*

Opposite: 4-TC trailer unit 420 leads another 4-TC and a 4-REP tractor unit approaching Vauxhall with a typical Waterloo – Bournemouth semi-fast working on a cold and damp January day in 1970. After three years the overall eggshell blue livery is looking the worse for wear and the two rear units have already been repainted in blue and grey. 420 was one of the last of its class to receive the later livery, being outshopped in September that year. *John H. Bird/www.anistr.com*

Although the Brush Type 4 diesels drafted in to help in the last days of Bournemouth line steam had a reputation for unreliability, on this occasion D1931 was not the culprit. On 29 March 1967, while working the 07.30 Weymouth to Waterloo, it was called upon to push 4-TC 405 into Southampton following the failure of push-pull fitted D6506.

An unidentified type HB large electro-diesel hauls a 3-TC + 4-TC on an up test working near Bevois Park, Southampton, in August 1968. Below: Type JB electro-diesel E6048 hauls a pair of 4-TC trailer units crossing Totton causeway with 09.25 Weymouth–Waterloo on 13 May 1967 The leading 4-TC has temporarily had its centre vehicles substituted by a buffet/restaurant car and trailer brake first destined for a 4-REP.
All: John H. Bird/www.anistr.com

4-TC 404 passes Winchfield leading a down Bournemouth service in about June 1967. 404 had previously been running as a three-car unit and, as shown by its pristine light grey roof, the trailer first has only just been added. To the right workmen busy themselves in what was Winchfield's goods yard. *Brian Stephenson*

Opposite top: Type JB electro-diesel E6042 propels a pair of 4-TC units passing Bevois Park freight yard with a southbound Bournemouth line service in early 1967. It will shortly turn sharp right past Northam Junction and proceed through Southampton tunnel into Southampton station. *Strathwood Library Collection*

Right: 4-REP tractor unit 3003 and a 4-TC trailer unit leave the reversing siding and enter the up through platform at Bournemouth with the front portion of a fast service to Waterloo, calling only at Southampton, in February 1968. In a few minutes another 4-TC will arrive from Weymouth, propelled by a push-pull fitted B.R.C.W. type 3, and attach to the rear of the London train. In the background, track has recently been cleared from the former steam shed.
John H. Bird/www.anistr.com

Our final view of the new order on the Bournemouth line shows 4-TC 406 leading an eleven-car TC formation, propelled by a type JB electro-diesel, on a Waterloo-Bournemouth fast service through the New Forest near Lyndhurst Road in May 1967.
John H. Bird/www.anistr.com

Opposite: Testing days over, the experimental 6-TC trailer unit was used from January 1966 until July 1967 on the Oxted line. It was then overhauled and painted blue at Eastleigh, after which it operated the rush-hour shuttle between Clapham Junction and Kensington Olympia, colloquially known as the 'Kenny Belle'. With its redundant end gangways now removed and plated-over, 601 is seen parked in Clapham Yard between duties on 21 February 1970. It was withdrawn after sustaining a buffer-stop collision at Kensington in June that year.
Chris Wilson Collection

Our second view of 'The Sussex Venturer' rail tour on Saturday 4 January 1969 shows Bulleid/Raworth 'booster' Co-Co locomotive 20001 at Newhaven Harbour quayside platform after arriving from Seaford. KA type 3 diesel 6565 was at the other end of the train for this section. 20001 was no stranger to this location; as shown in several images in this book, it was a regular on the Victoria – Newhaven boat trains almost throughout its career. This would, however, be its very last visit. *John H. Bird/www.anistr.com*

Type HA 'booster' electric locomotive E5020 stands at Charing Cross in charge of the L.C.G.B. 'Pas de Calais' charter, formed of Bulleid and B.R. steam stock, on 30 May 1965. Departing at 08.33, the tour ran via Chislehurst and Maidstone East to Folkestone Harbour, where participants boarded a ferry to Boulogne connecting with a steam-hauled run to Abbeville. This was the L.C.G.B.s first continental tour venture and was greatly oversubscribed. *Chris Wilson Collection*

5-BEL 3051 approaches Amberley with along the pretty Mid-Sussex route from Horsham to Littlehampton with the Southern Electric Group's 'Southern Belle' rail tour on 30 April 1972. The S.E.G. was privileged to hire a BEL unit on this, the final day of 'Brighton Belle' operation. Perhaps surprisingly given their weight, they had wide route-availability over most of the S.R. electric network and had been used for Royal and other specials throughout their career.
John H. Bird/www.anistr.com

Green-liveried 20002, the second Co-Co 'booster' locomotive and then with a few months left on regular duties, departs from the Windsor lines side of Waterloo heading the B.P.P.S. 'The Bulleid Commemorative Rail Tour' excursion on 8 June 1968. 20002 worked the train as far as Seaford, setting out via Twickenham, Hounslow, Clapham Junction, Brixton, Crystal Palace, East Croydon and the Quarry Line. *Chris Wilson Collection*

Right: This appears to be a real photographic rarity as the leading 4-COR 3150 displays a promotional headboard for a Victoria to Bognor Regis Butlin's Holiday Camp Express as it speeds past Billinghurst in September 1962. *David Ford Collection*

The R.C.T.S. hired 5-BEL 3053 for a 'Brighton Belle Commemorative' tour on 1 April 1972, but it was so oversubscribed that it was repeated on 8 April. On the first occasion the tour is seen at Eastbourne during a mid-afternoon break. This whole-day tour started from Waterloo, travelled down the Portsmouth 'Direct' line and then covered virtually all electrified lines in Sussex before returning to Victoria. There was plenty of time, therefore, to enjoy the delights of Pullman catering. The row of cars, not one of them a classic at that time, certainly dates the picture! *Colour Rail*

Our final view of 'Hornby' 20001 on the 'Sussex Venturer' rail tour shows it at the quiet coastal branch terminus at Seaford, having just arrived from Lewes. This tour was the final passenger duty for this locomotive before withdrawal. On 4 January 1969 there would doubtless have been a stiff wind blowing off the English Channel to encourage the tour participants back on to the warm steam-heated coaches quickly. **Colour Rail**

Another view of the S.E.G.s 'Southern Belle' charter on 30 April 1972 sees 5-BEL 3051 approaching Horsham from Three Bridges. Starting from Brighton at 12.20, the tour visited virtually all Central Division coastal lines and branches without venturing north of Three Bridges. Return to Brighton was at 16.47, a minute earlier than booked, after a very pleasant afternoon out. *John Scrace*

Opposite Bottom: A private charter for Gulf Oil draws into Eastleigh with E6106 suitably labelled by its sponsors on 4 May 1969. *John Bird/www.anistr.com*

Following conversion of the London Midland Region's D.C. Watford and North London lines from fourth to third-rail, it was possible for Southern electric units to work over them via the (unelectrified) connection between the two systems at Richmond. 4-COR 3135 is seen alongside a B.R Eastleigh-built L.M.R. unit under the 1966 Euston trainshed. The COR was working the 'Southern & North London Electric Train Tour' on 8 November 1970, run by the L.C.G.B. Croydon Branch. The following year, a '2-BIL Farewell' tour would also run into Euston. *Chris Wilson Collection*

Top: 4-SUB 4116, one of the first steel-bodied units and dating from 1946, leads a sister unit passing Woking with a Waterloo – Aldershot special for the Farnborough Air Show on 13 September 1964. Bottom: From the same footbridge, 4-EPB 5015 and pair of 2-HAPs are seen returning with the empty stock of another Farnborough air show special from Aldershot on the same date. There were many spare units available at off-peak times and weekends for special workings such as these, and the high capacity of SUBs and EPBs made them invaluable for moving large crowds. *Both: Brian Stephenson*

A second view of the R.C.T.S. 'Brighton Belle Commemorative' tour shows 5-BEL unit 3053 standing at Ore, the eastern extremity of the 1935 Eastbourne electrification scheme, on 1 April 1972. Ore was the first station out of Hastings on the Ashford line, and many electric services ran through to terminate here to reduce congestion at the main station. It was also the location of an electrical control room and carriage shed.
Chris Wilson Collection